THE MINDFUL CHRISTIAN

Cultivating a Life of
Intentionality, Openness, and Faith

THE MINDFUL
CHRISTIAN

DR. IRENE KRAEGEL

BROADLEAF BOOKS
MINNEAPOLIS

THE MINDFUL CHRISTIAN

Cultivating a Life of Intentionality, Openness, and Faith

30 29 28 27 26 25 24   1 2 3 4 5 6 7 8 9

All bible verses are taken from the New Revised Standard Version (NRSV)

Library of Congress Control Number: 2024942566 (print)

Cover image: mrs/gettyimages
Cover design: Olga Grlic

Hardcover ISBN: 978-1-5064-5861-8
eBook ISBN: 978-1-5064-5862-5
Paperback ISBN: 979-8-8898-3575-2

Dedicated with love to Ken and Milo,
who fill my moments with joy

God grant me the serenity
to accept the things I cannot change;
courage to change the things I can;
and wisdom to know the difference.

—*Reinhold Niebuhr* [1]

CONTENTS

The steadfast love of the Lord never ceases, his mercies never come to an end; they are new every morning; great is your faithfulness.

Lamentations 3:22–23

Silence of the heart is necessary so you can hear God everywhere — in the closing of the door, in the person who needs you, in the birds that sing, in the flowers, in the animals.

—*Mother Teresa*[1]

CHAPTER 1

MINDFULNESS IS BEING HERE, WHERE GOD IS

The word is near you, on your lips and in your heart.
Romans 10:8

The Act of Being Present

Mindfulness is the act of showing up, of being present for the life that God has given us.

Everyday mindlessness of ordinary moments can serve as a nudge toward mindfulness. Have you ever had one of the following experiences? Maybe a critical comment has looped in your head while you were trying to sleep. Maybe you've spaced out during a conversation and missed the most important part of what was said. Perhaps you've driven all the way from work to home without any awareness of the journey along the way. Or maybe you found yourself startled to look into the eyes of someone you love and realize you haven't actually *seen* them for a long time. If you have had any of these mindless experiences, then congratulations! You are human.

As it turns out, bringing awareness into the present moment is one of the hardest things for the adult human mind to do. Living in the moment comes more easily for very young children and also for animals, both of whom appear less consumed with the past and the future. But for the rest of us, it is natural to push through each day on autopilot as our thoughts cycle mindlessly on repeat, silently triggering emotional responses. Unaware of the body's physical signals, we can be preoccupied with past negative experiences and potential future disasters. This disconnection from our own moment-to-moment experience can leave us feeling powerless to change unpleasant feelings and fractured relationships, and we might struggle to see or understand the workings of our own hearts and minds, much less to see God's work in our midst.

The human experience in these modern times is often distracted, disconnected, and driven. With more technological convenience and digital communication, many of us have become more detached from the physical realities of our world as compared to past generations. We are less likely to feel the warmth of dishwater, see fireflies from the front porch, and have face-to-face interactions with one another. At the same time, we are increasingly exposed to a relentless flow of alarmist information and analysis, which pulls us into chronic, worried mental abstraction about our world. For those living in highly individualistic cultures, we have decreasing opportunities for communal connection and support. It is no wonder that mindfulness has become such a trend over the past decade. Our frenzied, anxious, detached souls are starved for calm and connection.

This is the gift of mindfulness—the cultivation of calm and connection through intentional awareness of the present moment. Mindfulness is learning to step out of frenzied mental abstraction in order to be *here*. Just like showing up for class, being *here* for life gives us the opportunity to learn and understand the lessons provided in each moment. Being *here* helps us to flourish and grow in wisdom, to calm agitated emotions, and to receive the good gifts that God has built into each moment of earthly existence. Being *here* helps us to be available to divine guidance, care, and revelation by paying attention to God's work. Being *here* is our doorway to joyful, abundant, resurrection life.

When we practice mindfulness, we cultivate an experience of the world as new, seeing things as if for the very first time. This fresh perspective helps us to be *here*, to be present. This is because first-time experiences have a particular richness to them, with an inherent ability to get our attention and boost our happiness levels as a result.

Recently, my friend's granddaughter had this type of first-time experience when she received new hearing aids at the age of twenty-six. Having had a severe hearing loss since birth, her response to newly perceived sounds was deeply emotional. She wrote in her private blog that the loudness of car locks, keyboard sounds, keys jangling, and toilets flushing all caught her by surprise. The sound of consonants was a thrill. Classical music was "incredible" and "three-dimensional." Her commentary about birds was especially moving: "I heard birdsong this morning for the first time in my life! Most of my walk was spent alternating between standing perfectly still to listen to the world and laughing/crying about the birds. I can still hardly believe it."

As I read her blog, I asked myself, *When was the last time that birdsong stopped me in my tracks while I laughed and cried in amazement?* Her mindful response to the experience of sound was an appropriate response to her encounter with God's creation. I now practice listening to birdsong with fresh ears on a regular basis, finding myself lost in amazement at such a delightful, musical, unearned gift in the midst of my everyday experience.

Mindfulness provides us with access to this type of amazement in response to the world, so that we can be transformed by an attitude of openness, wonder, and full attention. Mindfulness opens us up to the possibility of surprise and even joy as we practice being present to each moment as if we are experiencing it for the very first time. This practice of *presence* is invigorating, healing, and instructive, because it directs our attention to the space God inhabits: the present moment.

On its own, mindfulness is a powerful psychological tool, but it becomes especially powerful when combined with Christian faith because it readies us for divine connection. Over the past several years of practicing mindfulness within a Christian framework, I have experienced it as a conduit of God's joy, contentment, and peace. Mindfulness has helped me to build resilience, perseverance, hope, and courage in the midst of difficult circumstances, and it has given me a level of satisfaction that I've never known before. Along the way, mindfulness has revitalized my faith, opening me to experience God's presence in a deep and refreshing way.

In the pages of this book, I share my own journey of mindfulness and invite your participation in Christian mindfulness as well. Together we'll look at what mindfulness is and how it is practiced, and we will explore the connections between mindfulness and faith. Throughout the book, you'll also find an invitation to slow down and, if you choose, try out some basic practices. These engagements with the practice will be your best teacher as you consider the application of present-moment awareness in the Christian life.

Learning to Pay Attention

You might take an opportunity to pause here for a moment to notice where your mind is right now. Maybe you have a lot to think about; you may notice your thoughts wandering during the course of your reading. This is quite normal. Most of the time, our minds are not in the same place as our body. We ruminate about difficult memories from the past. (*What did that person mean by that comment? Why wasn't that handled differently? What if I had made a different decision?*) We ruminate about anticipated difficulties in the future. (*What if it's awful? What will people think of me? What if I can't handle it?*)

When we wander through the past and future with negativity, our minds can be the creators of much of their own suffering. It is easy to believe that thinking about past or future difficulties will help us, and occasionally it does help. More often, however, our thinking is stuck in unhelpful, critical loops that are outside our awareness. This looping creates problems that may not even exist and keeps us from solving problems that do exist, pulling us into painful emotions that are disconnected from the reality of the present moment.

Our thoughts, it turns out, often create more problems than they solve. When we step off the rushing train of thoughts in order to pay attention to the *now*, we discover that we actually have what we need in the moment, that we are okay. We also discover there are steps we can take in the moment to care effectively for ourselves.

As long as we are alive, we are thinking. Our brains generate thoughts, one after another, in much the same way that our hearts pump blood and our lungs breathe air. The goal of mindfulness is not to stop thinking or to clear the mind. Instead, the goal is to work skillfully with our thoughts, recognizing that thoughts are only one element of each moment. Thoughts do not control us, nor are they facts. They are simply experiences passing through the mind. Mindfulness gives us the means to decide what to do with these thought experiences and how to respond.

By cultivating this type of observational distance from thoughts, mindfulness helps increase awareness of present-moment experiences outside of our thoughts. And in each of these nonthought experiences, God is with us. God is present in the feeling of a breeze on skin, in the smile of a stranger, in that first sip of morning coffee, in the support of a chair. God creates and fills our moments with birdsong, the warmth of sunshine, glimmers of light on puddles of water. Each step we take is in God; each breath we take is a direct gift of the divine. While God sometimes speaks to us through our thoughts, God often communicates through these direct, nonthinking, physical experiences that, in turn, renew our thought life.

When we practice awareness of the present moment, we are practicing being with God, who is always here, always stable. But the instability of our attention means that staying with God in the present moment requires intentionality on our part. We have to connect with the present moment on purpose to avoid being pulled out of the present moment by mindless rumination.

One of the most powerful tools for this intentional process of mindful awareness is silence. For this reason, silent meditation is one of the cornerstones of mindfulness practice. Silent meditation helps us create just enough distance from our experience to become observers—observers of our own thoughts, feelings, physical sensations, behaviors, and urges. This observation of experience increases our awareness while decreasing the power that these experiences have over us in our mindless state. Sitting in mindful silence helps us become less muddled and more aware, thereby clearing space to perceive God at work in the moment. It helps open us to all that God has in store.

In the pages to come, we will explore the role of silent meditation as well as informal mindfulness practice, along with various definitions of mindfulness. Throughout this exploration, you will notice a particular attitude inherent to mindfulness: an attitude of both curiosity and kindness. This mindful attitude is friendly to our experience, simply noticing what is playing out in the present moment without rejecting it or clinging on. It is an open attitude that allows our experience to come and go, moment to moment, without judgment or harshness. Because the light and open quality of mindful attention is so central to the definition, we will return to that quality over and over throughout the course of this book.

Mindfulness is called a "practice" for a reason, as it is more of a recurring exercise than a permanent state of mind. Even the most seasoned meditators find their minds frequently wandering, so instead of expecting to "arrive" at a mindful state, we practice "returning"—coming back, over and over, to *this* place and to *this* moment. We give up expectations of any particular result, and we give up fruitless striving, trusting that God will do God's good work. Rather than trying to create a state of relaxation or calm through mindfulness practice, we practice being awake to whatever is in the moment. Whenever we notice that the mind has wandered off, we return to the present with gentleness and curiosity. We come back to the place where God is working in us—right here and right now—as we reconnect with our calm center.

If you would like, you can try this in the form of a micro-practice by pausing and noticing again where your mind is right now. Notice any expectant thoughts for this small practice, and simply become aware of what you think "should" happen as you try this out. If possible, observe your thoughts with light, curious, gentle attention, no matter what you are feeling, and notice that you are sitting in God's presence as you do this. This is Christian mindfulness—creating just enough observational distance to become aware of your experience in the present moment with kind awareness, recognizing that God is with you in that moment as part of your present-moment experience.

Now, as you reflect on the micro-practice, what did you observe? Was there any way in which that light, curious attention changed your perception of passing thoughts? There is no right or wrong answer here, it is simply a moment to notice. As we progress through these pages, you will have additional opportunities to dive into mindfulness practice at various levels if you so choose.

For Christian disciples, each micro-moment is where we are learning and practicing the rhythms of grace; this is where we have access to God's transforming presence. Whether we are enjoying the present moment or wishing it were different is irrelevant to its usefulness as a place of divine instruction. In the present moment, in the here and now, in the place where we are—this is where we are alive. And here is where we have the repeated opportunity to learn from our creator teacher. But such learning requires first that we show up, that we be present. This is the practice of mindfulness.

The Gift That Unlocked the Others

Perhaps you have a story about a time your life turned around for the better. For me, the discovery of mindfulness was that profound turnaround. At a point in my life when circumstances were quite good, I hit an all-time emotional low. Years of self-hatred and hopelessness rose to a powerful crescendo as I found myself lying in bed, sobbing, and wanting to die. I was in a loving marriage of many years and had a sweet and wonderful toddler, the fulfillment of years of longing and prayer. We had settled in a lovely home that fit us just right, a stability I treasured after years of moving. I was successful in my work, exercising regularly, consistent in my faith, and connected to many kind friends.

From the outside, everything seemed right. But on the inside, I had crumbled, and I didn't know what to do about it. I had already tried counseling, medication, prayer, and just plain old determination. There were seasons of reprieve but nothing long-lasting. When asked to name one time I had experienced happiness in my life, I couldn't think of a single example. Even when I was surrounded by happy circumstances, misery was my norm.

During this season, I was vulnerable enough to try something I had been skeptical about—mindfulness meditation. Having seen this practice so often presented in the context of Buddhism, I wasn't sure how it might fit with my deep commitment to Jesus. For me, there was nothing more important than my Christian faith. Yet as a clinical psychologist, I was hearing increasingly about the science of mindfulness as a new and effective form of treatment within the mental health field. I was fascinated by the treatment opportunities for the clients with whom I worked—clients experiencing similar feelings of depression, anxiety, and overall despair. Further, a deep longing inside of me drew me toward this practice. In my desperation for deep healing and wholeness, I began to suspect that mindfulness might hold an answer to my suffering and the suffering of my clients.

So I signed up for a mindfulness class and embarked on the experience with a blend of open-mindedness and guarded ambivalence. Early on in the practice of mindfulness meditation, I became aware of the depth of sadness within me. More surprisingly, I became aware of a constant stream of judgmental thoughts in my mind that were fueling my depressed feelings. Staying truly present to these sad emotions was incredibly challenging. In the process, I found myself drawing on past experiences of loss with the metaphor of hospice, recognizing the role of acceptance when encountering deep grief. As I did, I began to accept my depressed feelings. I knew I couldn't control them, and I had to give up any attachment to being "cured." Acknowledging this was a radically courageous and restorative step. It allowed me to let go of the struggle, to receive care, and to wholeheartedly embrace what was present. Ultimately, it allowed me to receive the gift wrapped within the suffering. But there was a true grieving process that also had to occur first.

As I had hoped, mindful acceptance of my emotions (even the depressed ones) indeed offered a pathway to well-being. Part of that well-being was a deep, enriching, refreshing, reviving sense of God's presence. While my mindfulness teacher said nothing about spirituality (her presentation of mindfulness practice was completely secular), it quickly became clear to me that God was at work in the practice.

As I took steps to sit in silence, become aware of the present moment, and let go of distracting thoughts, God's presence with me was palpable—not in the cognitive sense that I had known all along, but in a deep, abiding sense that warmed my heart and stirred my soul. Resting in mindful meditation, I became reacquainted with Jesus. I found myself moved to tears by the sweetness of his presence and filled with peaceful contentment as I sensed a divine invitation to sit at his feet. Even when my thoughts and feelings were a miserable jumble, mindfulness meditation became a tool to cut through the mental distractions and experience God. What began as a "secular" tool turned out to be a deeply "sacred" tool in the presence of the Master.

This experience of mindfulness meditation led me to a melded understanding of mindfulness and faith. God was at work in my life, and God used mindfulness to accomplish that work. I came to recognize mindfulness as an innate ability that God created in us to to clear the mental fog and experience the divine. In the same way that other gifts nourish us in our faith and health—food and water, exercise and medicine, reading and prayer, shelter and clothing, friends and family, speech and hearing—mindfulness is another nourishing gift. And in my case, it turned out to be the gift that unlocked the others. By learning the practice of present-moment awareness, I was enabled to receive other good gifts from God.

Since that first foray into mindfulness practice, my life has never been the same. I now know what happiness feels like, and I have no trouble remembering many times of happy feelings. While depression still pays me visits, it no longer sucks the life out of me or dominates my everyday experience. I have a much different relationship with depressed feelings, and I have specific tools to use in moving through them—a change for which I am deeply grateful to God. In the process, I have come to recognize the practice of present-moment awareness as deeply embedded in Scripture and in the Christian tradition. Called by many other names, mindfulness is a practice resonant throughout the history of Christianity for those who seek communion with God. For me, although mindfulness is not an easy tool or a quick fix, it has been a conduit of healing as I have learned to pay attention to the only place I can experience God: the present moment.

Because of my own passion for both Christian faith and mindfulness meditation, I am also passionate about exploring the blend of the two. This book has afforded me the opportunity to explore this blending with you, viewing mindfulness practice through the lens of faith.

If you are a Christ-follower experiencing emotional pain, spiritual lethargy, or feelings of disconnection, or if you are simply curious about how mindfulness can help you live a deeper life while also fitting with Christian faith, this book is for you. As we travel through the practice together, we'll look at practical applications of mindfulness to different aspects of our lives (for instance, eating mindfully). Ultimately, my goal for this book is to equip you to engage the ancient healing practice of mindfulness within a Christian framework in order to live joyfully and wholeheartedly in this world that God created.

Mindfulness Is Being Here, Where God Is

Living the Practice: Tuning In to the Senses

Choose one physical sense—hearing, touching, tasting, smelling, or seeing—and take time to pay careful attention to it throughout the day. For example, if you choose the sense of hearing, you might begin to notice passing sounds; if you choose the sense of sight, you may notice shapes and colors around you; if you choose the sense of touch, notice sensations on your skin (such as the feel of clothing, air, or how your skin feels in contact with surfaces as you sit in a chair). Each time you tune in to that particular physical sense, imagine that you have never encountered it before. Be curious about what it is like to experience this sense as if for the very first time. You can structure your practice in any one of the following three ways:

1. Choose one specific activity during which you will pay attention to the particular sensory experience that you have chosen. For example, you might walk around the block, wash the dishes, or weed a garden bed. During this activity, focus in on the particular type of sensory experience that you have chosen.

2. Set a timer and sit in silence, just noticing the sensory experience that you have chosen, until the timer rings.

3. As often as you remember during the day, turn your attention toward the specific sensory experience that you have chosen. To remind yourself to return to this awareness throughout the day, you might set a watch or phone alarm to repeat at regular intervals.

13

As you practice curious observation of your chosen sensory experience, be consciously aware of what you notice. You don't need to put language around the experience, analyze what is going on, or draw any conclusions. Just stay aware. See if it is possible to remove the filter of language and thought, having the experience directly rather than becoming attached to thoughts about it. When thoughts arise (which they will throughout the practice), notice that they are there, and then gently bring your awareness back to the sensory experience.

If it feels helpful, you may want to take time at the end of the practice to jot down some observations about your experience, cultivating an attitude of curiosity about what you noticed. ■

We are only the light bulbs . . . ,
and our job is just to remain screwed in.

—*Desmond Tutu*[1]

CHAPTER 2

RENEWING THE MIND, EASING SUFFERING

I shall see the goodness of the Lord in the land of the living.
Psalm 27:13

As mindfulness has become popularized, many expressions of the practice have sprung up over time. This can create some confusion about what people are referring to when they talk about mindfulness practice.

Let's start with what mindfulness is not. It is not progressive muscle relaxation, deep breathing, calmness, guided imagery, Transcendental Meditation, or Buddhism. It does not require sitting in particular positions or using particular meditation gear. Mindfulness is not a practice reserved for particular cultural, ethnic, socioeconomic, religious, or age groups. It is available for free to anyone who desires a happier, deeper, more connected, and more compassionate life.

Here is a nutshell definition. Mindfulness is the practice of paying attention to the present moment with intentionality, openness, and nonjudgmental curiosity—a direct awareness of experience as it unfolds, moment by moment. Through the practice of mindfulness, the "muscle" of attention is exercised in order to focus intentionally on the only moment in which there is any control: right now. While mindful awareness can be practiced on an informal basis throughout each day, focused attention to the moment is cultivated more deeply through periods of silent, formal meditation.

Mindful awareness provides us with the opportunity to be *in* our lives as something to be lived and experienced, not just something to be watched, documented, or evaluated by others. It allows us to stop living life as a performance and to start living life in flow with God's spirit. Mindfulness provides a connection to our creatureliness, to our existence as created beings in a vast created universe—an opportunity to feel part of something larger than ourselves, to experience ourselves as cared for and interconnected and whole. It decreases our sense of fragmentation and misery in an increasingly fragmented world. It helps us to cut through the noise of the information age in order to attend to the things that matter, and to care well for our souls in the process.

Here are some additional definitions of mindfulness that resonate with me. "Mindfulness is simply being aware of what is happening right now without wishing it were different; enjoying the pleasant without holding on when it changes (which it will); being with the unpleasant without fearing it will always be this way (which it won't)."[2] "Mindfulness means paying attention to what is happening right now with kindness and curiosity—paying attention in a way that helps you live a happier life."[3]

Mindfulness is not a rigid, formal system, and children are sometimes able to describe it best. This definition (paraphrased) came from my son at age six, and it may be the most accurate I have heard yet:

Sometimes we have an emotion that seems "bad," like anger, so we try to get away from that emotion and hide from it. While we're hiding, that emotion is just wandering around and not going away, and we're feeling scared of it. When we decide to come out of hiding and walk along together with that emotion, we find out that it is not so "bad" or "scary," and we start to feel better.

In all mindfulness practices, both formal and informal, the consistent theme is present-moment awareness. We use the word *practice* because that is exactly what is happening during these exercises—practicing present-moment awareness. There is not a particular goal toward which to strive during mindfulness practice, and there is nothing to prove or achieve, such as calmness or relaxation. We are simply waking up to whatever is there in the moment, practicing present-moment wakefulness.

In physical exercise, a person works the same muscle repeatedly in order to build strength and skill. In mindfulness practice, a person works the "muscle" of attention repeatedly in order to develop strength and skill. They practice noticing that the attention has moved away from the present moment, and each time they notice, they bring the attention back to where it was intended to be. The attention inevitably drifts away from the present moment over and over. Each time the person notices this has occurred, they return awareness to what is present in the moment. They practice having experiences directly, rather than diluting their experiences through the filters of language and thought.

Mindfulness practices do not involve "emptying" the mind or "clearing" thoughts. As long as we are alive, our brain will generate an endless stream of thoughts. Sometimes these thoughts are quieter, sometimes louder. Sometimes they are slow like a drizzle; other times they are fast and loud like a torrential downpour. But there is no denying that thoughts are always present. So during mindfulness meditation, we simply practice noticing the thoughts and becoming curious about them. We become aware of our emotional and physical reactions to certain thoughts, gathering information about the interactions between our minds, bodies, emotions, and behaviors. We learn to watch our constantly changing experiences from moment to moment.

Part of mindfulness practice is a particular attitude toward present-moment experience. Cultivating an attitude of playfulness and gentleness, the practitioner observes the moment without judgment (positive or negative) in order to gather information. This creates a bit of distance from experience, including from thoughts and feelings. For some, it is helpful to imagine these experiences passing before them like a movie or like clouds in the sky. For others, it can be useful to imagine walking up to a balcony or ascending in an elevator to get the bigger picture.

Through this process of mindful observation, we can practice stepping away from the stories and narratives we constantly and often unconsciously tell ourselves. Becoming more aware of the thought stream, we remove the layers of analysis and interpretation that cloud our direct experience. This decreases the grip of thoughts that pull away from God, shedding light on unconscious barriers to life in the Spirit. In this way, mindfulness provides an opportunity to get quiet enough to bring full attention to the only place we can ever meet God: the present moment.

The observational distance inherent in mindfulness practice has implications for the use of language. As you read this book or others about mindfulness, you may notice an unusual use of the word *the*, as in "the breath." For those new to mindfulness practice, this may sound odd. In typical American parlance, we describe experiences by using possessive adjectives—words like *my, your,* and *their*. For example, when referring to my experience of breathing, I would be much more likely in my daily discourse to say "my breath" rather than "the breath." This use of language gives us a sense of ownership over experiences, pulling them into the core of our personal identity and forming a strong connection. Through this common possessive language, we claim these passing experiences as part of who we are.

In mindfulness practice, we practice a shifted relationship to experience, and our language reflects this. No longer is a thought "mine," and a challenging physical sensation is no longer "my pain." Instead, we use language to cultivate observational distance between our identity and our passing experiences; one might refer to "thoughts passing through the mind" or "sensations in the body." This intentional shift supports the ability to be curious about present-moment experiences without becoming entangled in the ownership of the experiences. Letting go of ownership is an acknowledgment that the breath in my body is not my own but given to me by a power greater than myself—a divine gift shared with all breathing beings.

Renewal of the Mind

Having defined mindfulness in a broad sense, we can now contextualize the practice within a Christian framework. Both mindfulness and Christian tradition encourage intentionality about thoughts. Christian discipleship involves awareness of our inner life, the ability to know our thoughts so that we can present them to God for renewal. Because of this, Scripture invites us to "take captive every thought to make it obedient to Christ" (2 Cor 10:5), and "watch over your heart with all diligence, for from it flow the springs of life" (Prov 4:23). This intentional approach to our inner life is a prerequisite for mental transformation, summarized in the book of Romans: "Do not be conformed to this world, but be transformed by the renewal of your minds" (Rom 12:2).

Bible verses such as these remind us that there are significant limits to human perception. An even more direct statement about this is made in the book of Isaiah, where God points out, "My thoughts are not your thoughts, nor are your ways my ways" (Isa 55:8). Being a finite human being makes it difficult to move thoughts out of self-orbit, see truth, and perceive God's kingdom work in the world. Thinking patterns can become destructive; our own behaviors can confound us. While the gospel is clear that all is forgiven, the temptation to try to prove ourselves worthy is strong. In the language of mindfulness, the mind can be a dangerous place.

Thinking is not a bad thing. It is an essential component of human life, and it is one of the ways we reflect God's image. Thinking often serves us well, especially when we are intentional about cultivating healthy thinking patterns. So mindfulness is not about clearing the mind or stopping thoughts; it helps us become *more* aware of thoughts, not less. It changes our relationship to thoughts. The observational distance of mindfulness is for the purpose of increasing a sense of grounding in reality, not facilitating a dissociative state.

However, thinking becomes unhelpful (or even harmful) when it dissolves into undetected mental wandering. This kind of rumination sparks emotional pain and clouds our thinking, distracting us from effective coping in the moment. And given that we have no control outside of the present moment, it diminishes our problem-solving abilities by focusing us on the past and future—places where we have no direct control.

Thinking also can be painful when we fall into repetitive questions that do not have answers, especially when these questions relate to our own worth or success. Most "why" questions fall in this category, along with most "what's wrong with me" questions. No amount of logic can resolve questions like "Why did this happen to me?" or "What's wrong with me?" We ask those questions because we are longing for something deeper and more healing than a logical response. Through the practice of mindfulness, we move away from trying to figure it all out logically, and we open ourselves to an experience of God's presence, an experience that replaces the anxious questions with deeper truths of provision and grace.

On a spiritual level, this tendency to mentally wander through the past and imagined future creates distance between ourselves and God. When we don't show up for the moment, we are less likely to notice God with us (Matt 1:23). Mental noise about things past or future easily crowds out God's "still small voice" in the moment, in the quiet of the heart. This may explain why God repeated the assuring command throughout Scripture: "Do not worry" (Matt 6:25; Phil 4:6). An uncluttered mind increases one's capacity to draw close to and hear God, receiving the divine gifts offered in the moment.

Mindfulness presents an alternative to the aimless rumination of worry, increasing intentionality about thoughts to support the "renewal of the mind" spoken of in the book of Romans. Again, this is different from trying to stop thoughts or to change them into something different. Resistance to negative thoughts tends to backfire by locking us into ongoing engagement with them, even as the mind tries to reason its way out.

Mindfulness practice, in contrast, leads to becoming more aware of specific thoughts in the mind and then releasing the grip on them, opening the practitioner to God's loving renewal. In this practice, we accept that our thoughts are ever present but not ever true, learning to watch them come and go with curiosity and even a sense of humor.

For example, in a moment when I am beating myself up about a less-than-stellar presentation at work, I might start by noticing my thought stream—naming the thoughts (without judging or suppressing them) and smiling at them with lighthearted attention. I then become curious about my experience surrounding the thoughts, asking questions such as these: *What other thoughts are present in this moment? What physical sensations do I notice in my body as I think this? Is there muscle tension, a shift in the breath pattern, quickening of the heartbeat, clenching in the gut? What urges emerge for me in conjunction with these thoughts—perhaps the urge to quit my job or eat a large bowl of ice cream?* As a Christian practitioner of mindfulness, I also open my awareness to acknowledge God's presence with me in that moment of pain, becoming aware of God as an integral part of my experience.

Through a mindful process such as this, the practitioner expands awareness as a method of diluting the strength of unhelpful thoughts. You might imagine thoughts in the mind as salt. When one teaspoon of salt is diluted in a small cup of water, the taste is overpowering and bitter. But pour that salty solution into a barrel of water, and you won't taste the salt at all. It's still there, but increasing the water dilutes the taste and makes it palatable. So it is with mindful awareness of thoughts, which effectively expands awareness beyond unhelpful thoughts to reduce their power.

In this way, mindfulness becomes a partnership between us and God. We do the courageous work of pausing, getting quiet, becoming aware, and observing thoughts nonjudgmentally. This disengages us from attachments to our own perceptions, creating space for God to do the work of restoration, transformation, and healing. Rather than resisting or arguing with thoughts, we become aware that the thoughts are not the only thing in our experience of that moment, and not necessarily the truest thing. In the process, God expands our vision, and we find ourselves grounded in something that is much larger than ourselves and much truer.

Working with Suffering

If mindfulness theory emphasizes working skillfully with thoughts as a key element of managing suffering, how does this fit within a Christian worldview of pain? Both mindfulness and Christianity acknowledge pain as an inherent part of the human journey, and both extend hope for easing that pain. Interestingly, both also encourage an approach to suffering that is open rather than resistant. Let's look at how this shows up in the two traditions.

Christianity views suffering in the context of God's work in our lives. At times, God uses healing power to ease our suffering. At other times, healing does not remove pain in the way we might hope, but God teaches, shapes, and transforms us along the path of suffering. Suffering is used by God to build our character and draw us into a closer relationship. Christians need not fear pain, knowing that God will always provide for us and bring good out of suffering.

Because of this openness that Christianity cultivates toward God's work in all circumstances (even the painful ones), the Christian is well prepared to engage with mindfulness practice around suffering. Mindfulness is one of the tools that God has given us to drop our resistance and open ourselves to God's healing presence during times of pain—a straightforward system of self-monitoring within us. The mindfulness practitioner accepts all experiences, whether liked or disliked, and watches to see how those experiences change over time. The Christian mindfulness practitioner cultivating this nonreactive observance of suffering can do so with an awareness that God is at work in the process.

The God-given power of mindfulness to ease suffering has a neurological basis. Brain scans show that mindfulness practitioners experience a thickening of connective tissue between emotional and rational areas of the brain. In addition, emotional centers become smaller. These changes increase the ability of mindfulness meditators to moderate intense emotions—to pause before reacting, blending emotions with rational thought in a skillful manner that reduces stress and suffering.[4] Mindfulness practitioners do not experience less emotion; instead, their brain structures become more supportive of effective and calm responses to their emotions so that they do not remain stuck in chronically uncomfortable emotional states. For this reason, mindfulness has emerged as a leading treatment for depression, with research showing that it is just as effective as antidepressant medication for preventing relapse of major depressive episodes.[5]

Along with emotional suffering, mindfulness practice also reduces physical suffering. The negative impact of overthinking our physical pain is visible in brain scans, with a good example of this found in the biology of chronic pain. Research shows that chronic pain tends to light up the entire brain in MRI scans. As the somatosensory areas of the brain are activated, other areas of the brain (such as the emotionally charged limbic system) also are activated in response to that pain. But when we practice meditation, the brain learns to quiet down in response to pain. This means that the somatosensory areas may or may not continue to light up in MRI scans (meditation does not always remove the physical sensations of pain), but the rest of the brain becomes quieter, and negative emotions in response to the sensory pain experience are lessened. As the mindfulness practitioner develops less reactive methods of working with physical sensations, their relationship with pain is changed, and their overall level of suffering is reduced.[6]

To help understand this neurological basis for the impact of mindfulness meditation on the pain experience, I offer a personal example of mindfulness used to manage physical pain. When I have a headache, there is a stream of commentary accompanying it—something like this: *This is awful. How am I supposed to get through a workday feeling like this? I'm such a wimp. Life is too hard.* Not surprisingly, these thoughts do not help my headache feel better, and they do not support positive emotions. In fact, they are likely to trigger increased physical tension, adding to my discomfort.

However, when I'm able to practice mindfulness in that moment of physical pain, I notice a change. This starts by first becoming aware that I am suffering and allowing myself to say "ouch," turning toward myself as I would toward a friend or a small child who is hurting. In this moment of mindfulness, I notice my self-critical thoughts as symptoms of suffering, rather than facts. That in turn allows me to notice other things in the moment, such as these:

- The direct *sensations* in my head, and the option to use descriptions of them besides "pain." Perhaps I notice tightness, tension, pulsing, or pressure. Perhaps I become aware that each sensation has a shape and size, with variations that change from one moment to the next. These observations help to create a more direct experience of physical sensation, moving beyond interpretations to a more direct and nuanced description.

- The *thoughts* present in my mind related to the headache. I might create a little distance from thoughts passing through the mind, becoming aware of their pace and speed as I get specific about each separate cognition. Perhaps I suspend judgment about whether each thought is true and see if it is possible to observe my thoughts with a bit of humor, noticing the somewhat comic tendency of my mind to instantly spin into hopeless self-judgment in response to pain.

- The *emotions/feelings* that are present for me. Perhaps there is anxiety, anger, or disappointment. There's no need for me to explain these emotions or justify them. I can just notice what emotions are arising in the moment, holding them with kindness and compassion. I can practice seeing myself through God's eyes as someone in need of care during a moment of suffering.

- The *urges and behaviors* in response to physical sensation. Perhaps I observe my escape impulse as one that is familiar during moments of suffering. I might notice the option to ride the waves of these urges without automatically giving in, taking good care of myself in the midst of the physical and emotional discomfort.

When I practice this type of mindful curiosity in response to pain, I use my brain in different ways than I would in auto-pilot. No longer am I lost in an unobserved, mindless thought stream that exacerbates my suffering. Instead, I am now shifting how my brain works by connecting the emotional and rational centers of activity. I am strengthening the logical, rational areas of my brain while reducing the control of my brain's emotional, fight-or-flight limbic system. This is an intentional activation of a God-given mechanism for reducing suffering—the mechanism of mindful attention.

Receiving the Breath

A hallmark of any mindfulness practice is increasing observation of specific thoughts while also expanding awareness beyond the mind. So if we choose to shift our focus elsewhere, to move beyond thoughts, where else might we attend? There are many choices, and we will explore these different options throughout the book, including their place within formal mindfulness practices. But let's begin here where so much of mindfulness practice begins: with the breath as an object of awareness.

Being aware of our breath, or practicing "breath awareness," is often used to move attention beyond thoughts, to get us in touch with emotion, and to activate the body's natural calming mechanisms. Paying attention to breath can move us out of a mindless, agitated swirl of mental activity into a more centered, present-moment experience of the body. Some mindfulness practitioners even relate to the breath as a "friend" to which they learn to return again and again, describing a sense of comfort in knowing that the breath is always with them.

Breath is powerful. From the earliest words of Scripture, we know that God used breath to create life, changing the first man from a pile of dust into a living human (Gen 2:7). Jesus used breath to impart the Holy Spirit to the disciples (John 20:22). And Scripture itself is God-breathed (2 Tim 3:16). So when we breathe, which we do as long as we are alive, we are participating in divine work. We are receiving a gift from our creator that has literally been passed down from one generation to the next, from the time God first breathed into Adam. Given by God, breath is a sacred gift.

God's breath courses through every moment of our lives. God's essence is woven into the very fabric of our physical being; without this gift of breath, we cannot survive. When we tune in to our breath, paying attention to the physical sensations of breathing, we are tuning in to the life-giving force of God. We are recognizing our connection to divine work, our total God-dependence. By ourselves, we cannot make the breath happen. We can only become aware of breathing as a sacred gift.

It is wondrous that God's divine presence is attached to such a constant, elemental, earthy component of our existence, much like the institution of Holy Communion and its basic elements of bread and wine. God did not simply say, "Think about my sacrifice on the cross for you." Instead, God attached the memory of that sacrifice to an everyday meal. In this way, we have the opportunity to recognize God in the life-giving force of food: we can remember Christ's love and sacrifice each day in the energy and nourishment of food and drink.[7] So it is with breath awareness. In this simple noticing of the in-breath and the out-breath, we find hints of God. By recognizing the divine sustenance of each breath, provided in each moment without any effort on our part, we have the opportunity to recognize God's spirit at work in our lives.

Many people find breath awareness to be calming, but for some, it might feel uncomfortable or even panic inducing. There are other ways to practice mindfulness, and it's perfectly fine to acknowledge this discomfort and choose another object of attention besides the breath. In fact, moving attention away from the breath can be a very mindful action if done with intentionality. Remember, the goal of mindfulness is simply to notice what one is doing with the mind as one does it. Mindful practice is not meant to be applied as a rigid set of rules, and it does not require one to force the attention into remaining in a place that causes distress. Instead, it is meant to be modified to fit your needs in the moment. So use breath awareness as it is helpful, and leave what is unhelpful. This is an act of self-care.

Whatever your experience while observing the breath, expect surprises along the way. Each breath is new, each emotion is new, and each moment is new, so one can be prepared for a variety of experiences with the breath and allow new experiences and perceptions about breath awareness to emerge over time. For every moment of life, God is providing breath and doing new things. We only need to watch with openness and curiosity as we ground ourselves in our present-moment experiences through the practice of mindfulness.

An Invitation to Awareness

In Scripture, the book of 1 Kings tells the story of Elijah, a prophet used by God to silence the prophets of the false god Baal in a miraculous and noisy display of fiery power. After this amazing victory for Elijah and God's devoted followers, Elijah is quickly driven into hiding by the evil Queen Jezebel. He is left empty, bitter, and suicidal, consumed by hopeless thoughts. God meets Elijah in this place of despair, using a method that could easily have been missed: silence. We hear about the lead-up to this moment of silence in the following Old Testament narrative:

> [The Lord] said, "Go out and stand on the mountain before the Lord, for the Lord is about to pass by." Now there was a great wind, so strong that it was splitting mountains and breaking rocks in pieces before the Lord, but the Lord was not in the wind; and after the wind an earthquake, but the Lord was not in the earthquake; and after the earthquake a fire, but the Lord was not in the fire; and after the fire a sound of sheer silence. When Elijah heard it, he wrapped his face in his mantle and went out and stood at the entrance of the cave. Then there came a voice to him that said, "What are you doing here, Elijah?" (1 Kgs 19:11–13)

This is a moment of mindfulness for Elijah—a moment of silence that does not require anything except showing up and listening. When Elijah walks to the entrance of the cave, God is not looking to him for in-depth thought or analysis, not asking Elijah to prove anything or to do anything spectacular. In this meeting, God asks only for Elijah to show up at the entrance to the cave and practice basic awareness: "What are you doing here, Elijah?"

Early in my mindfulness training, I had a similar God-encounter. The first time I went to a mindfulness meditation class, the instructor invited us to sit upright, close our eyes, breathe, and enter silence. I sat silent, uncomfortable, apprehensive, resistant, cynical. She posed one simple question: "What brought you here?"

In resistance, my busy thoughts responded, *This is so cheesy! I hate forced exercises like this.*

A moment later, she asked again, "What really brought you here?"

What brought me here? What really brought me here? I finally asked myself. What I became aware of was a palpable feeling of sadness in my heart cavity, in the thought mill of my mind, and in every cell of my body.

Once more the instructor asked, "What really, really, really brought you here?"

In that moment, I knew. I was depressed and hopeless, at the end of my rope. I was desperately hoping that learning mindfulness would be the answer. Until that point, I had felt miserable but hadn't leaned directly into the sadness with an attitude of openness, curiosity, and nonjudgment. That moment of direct connection with my sad emotion allowed me to experience an unexpected surge of kind attention toward myself, to see myself, tenderly, as a child of God.

In that mindful moment of full awareness, there was a new clarity. Like Elijah, I heard God's call in the silence and showed up at the entrance of the cave. I heard the invitation to full awareness—"What are you doing here?"—and I laid down my resistance, opening the door to God's hope and healing. This was the beginning of a transformational, healing process for me.

Christian mindfulness is showing up where God is, in the present moment, and paying attention to all that is in that given moment so as not to miss God's renewal and healing. It is cultivating silent spaces for listening and awareness, releasing our tight grip on thoughts in order to open our hands to all that God provides in the moment. It is receiving from God the continually miraculous gift of breath with intentionality, laying down human resistance to reality as it is, and leaning into the moment in full faith that God provides.

God is at work, with or without our mindful awareness in each moment. But in the words of Annie Dillard, "Beauty and grace are performed whether or not we will sense them. The least we can do is try to be there. . . . Otherwise, creation would be playing to an empty house."[8]

Living the Practice: Standing at the Cave Entrance

As you consider embarking on this journey of mindfulness, set aside some time to show up at the entrance of the cave, as did Elijah. Find a space where you can have uninterrupted quiet, and settle into a physical posture that supports a sense of wakeful awareness. Whether or not you "feel" anything spiritual, acknowledge that God is present in the silence.

As you come to stillness, ask yourself this simple question posed by God to Elijah: "What are you doing here?" Insert your own name at the end, making the question personal. Then listen, observe, and attend with an attitude of openness and curiosity about what God will reveal in the quiet space. Consider repeating the question to yourself a couple more times, leaving long stretches in between to cultivate gentle awareness of your thoughts and feelings.

Nothing in particular needs to happen in these moments of silence. You may notice emotion that is pleasant, unpleasant, or neutral. You may find that your mind is busy and distracted, or you may experience cognitive quietness and peace. Perhaps longings emerge quickly, or you might sit with the question over a long period of time before gaining some clarity. There is nothing you need to do here at the cave's entrance, other than to be present and trust emergence.

God is in the silence. We only need to observe and listen with an openness to divine presence, to enter into an attitude of being rather than doing, and then to cultivate curiosity about what will happen as we meet God there. ■

We are all of us from birth to death guests at a table which we did not spread. The sun, the earth, love, friends, our very breath are parts of the banquet. . . . Shall we think of the day as a chance to come nearer to our Host, and to find out something of Him who has fed us so long?

—*Rebecca Harding Davis*[1]

CHAPTER 3

MINDFULNESS WITHIN CHRISTIAN TRADITION

The earth is the Lord's and all that is in it,
the world, and those who live in it.

Psalm 24:1

Present-Moment Awareness and Christianity

Throughout all major world religions, evidence of the practice of present-moment awareness appears in some form. The ability to focus attention on the here and now is an ancient and innate approach to spirituality, as it helps us hear truths deeper than the thoughts coursing through our minds at every waking moment. Because of this, you can find direct explorations of present-moment awareness as a spiritual discipline within a variety of Christian traditions throughout history. Let's look at some of these traditions together.

During the third, fourth, and fifth centuries, Desert Mothers and Fathers retreated into the desert to practice present-moment awareness. While some lived as isolated hermits and others lived embedded in community, all believed that God was actively at work through times of intentional silence. These hermits believed that controlling one's thoughts was a primary method of preventing and caring for soul sickness, of "guarding the heart." And they did this by practicing awareness of thoughts in the mind while setting those thoughts free to be transformed by God. By becoming aware of and curious about their thoughts while noticing which thoughts were more and less helpful, they increased their ability to open their minds to God's shaping over time.

During the Middle Ages, numerous mystics explored ways to relate to God that moved beyond language, thought, interpretation, or preconceived ideas—a state of being they often termed "unity with God." Meister Eckhart, for example, encouraged a direct loving of God without the intermediaries of mental activity, images, and representations.[2] The anonymous author of The Cloud of Unknowing explored God as a pure entity beyond any human capacity of mental conception.

In the sixteenth century, Saint Ignatius established the Society of Jesus—the Jesuits, a Roman Catholic order continuing to this day. At the core of his theology, Ignatius affirmed "God in all things." He taught that by paying attention to every part of life, we have the opportunity to find God. This type of attentiveness to God was meant to be cultivated both in life's moment-to-moment experiences and also in times of contemplative meditation. Ignatius also taught the practice of "indifference"—training the mind to let go of attachments to things, thoughts, and outcomes. One classic contemplative text springing out of the Jesuit tradition is The

Sacrament of the Present Moment by Jean-Pierre de Caussade.[3]
A beautiful introduction to the Jesuit tradition in modern times,
replete with overlapping principles of mindfulness, can be found in
James Martin's book A Jesuit Guide to (Almost) Everything.[4]

Throughout the ages, these Christian traditions have pointed
us to the reality of God's work in silence and God's presence in
the everyday moments of our lives, including the moments that
are painful and uncomfortable. Each is a classic spiritual tradition
worthy of engagement in its own right, with foundational truths
about present-moment awareness that support the modern-day
application of mindfulness within a Christian framework.

Mindfully Meditative Christian Practices

In light of this historical overview, let's now explore some specific
meditative practices of Christian devotion that have become
common in modern times. These are not identical to traditional,
formal mindfulness practices; an introduction to more standard
practices will be presented in the next chapter. But each one of
these Christian practices has significant overlap with the practice
of mindfulness meditation.

CENTERING PRAYER

Three Trappist monks in the 1970s drew on centuries of Christian
contemplative tradition to formalize a practice of present-moment
awareness called Centering Prayer.[5] This is a silent practice of
tuning attention to God's presence in the moment.

Within a Christian worldview, Centering Prayer can be viewed
as a type of mindfulness meditation that focuses on God as the
object of moment-to-moment awareness. This is an adaptation of
the practice of focusing on elements of the present moment, such as
breath, physical sensations, or thoughts. Practitioners of Centering

Prayer choose another element of the present moment—God—as the focus of their awareness during meditation.

The following four steps offer a guide for engagement with the practice of Centering Prayer:[6]

1. Choose a prompt for your attention during the practice. This could be a "sacred word" (such as peace or Father) or a "sacred breath" that you attend to as a reminder of God's presence. Then set a timer for twenty minutes.

2. Sit in a comfortable but alert manner. Close your eyes, if you choose, and settle your attention on the near presence of God, within you or in the room. As a sign of consent to God's presence, introduce your chosen prompt in your mind.

3. Quietly and lightly repeat the sacred word in the background of your awareness, using it as a prompt to bring your attention back to God's presence, or simply use your breath for this purpose. (The latter is more consistent with typical mindfulness practice.) When you find yourself distracted by thoughts, feelings, or physical sensations, gently return your awareness once again to God's presence.

4. When the timer goes off, remain with eyes closed for approximately two minutes as you transition out of silence into the rest of your day, bringing the experience of God's presence along with you.

LECTIO DIVINA

Lectio divina is an ancient Benedictine meditative practice. Translated as "divine reading," this prayerful engagement with Scripture is one way of centering our attention on biblical words in order to open our hearts to God's present-moment movement in our souls. While lectio divina is often facilitated in a group context, it can also be practiced in solitude.

After choosing a brief passage of Scripture (often one to two verses) as your focus, the practice of lectio divina has four basic steps:

1. Read the passage out loud. Allow your mind to understand the words, to comprehend their meaning, and to rest in them. Get to know the passage. You may wish to read the passage aloud several times.

2. Meditate on the passage. Chew it over, use your imagination, and envision yourself in the midst of it. Open your heart to receive whatever God might have for you in the passage at this moment.

3. Respond to the passage. Notice if a word or phrase speaks to you, and say this out loud or write it in a journal. Acknowledge what the passage is saying to you, and talk to God about it.

4. Rest in the passage. Sit in silence, resting in *being* mode rather than *doing* mode. Allow God to work without effort on your part. Attend and listen.

LISTENING PRAYER

Listening (or contemplative) prayer is the practice of bringing direct awareness to God's presence and listening to God with intentionality. Listening prayer often involves sitting before God in attentive silence, but it can also be practiced on an ongoing basis throughout the course of one's day. There is no standardized format for listening prayer.

Listening prayer can be traced throughout Christian tradition as a practice of being present to God.[7] One well-known proponent of this type of contemplative prayer practice was Brother Lawrence of the Resurrection, a humble lay brother in a Carmelite monastery during the seventeenth century. He described his prayer life as "simple attention" to God's presence throughout the mundane and ordinary moments of each day, and his thoughts on the topic were summarized after his death in what has become a classic and beloved spiritual text, The Practice of the Presence of God.[8]

Listening prayer, like most mindfulness meditation, is largely a wordless practice. It does not involve forming thoughts and statements to project in God's direction. Rather, it draws the practitioner into the present moment as an attentional exercise. The attitude of listening prayer acknowledges the temptation for humans to fill prayer with thoughts, words, and agendas, talking at God with no direct awareness of God's presence and no expectation of a response. The goal of this practice is instead to listen for what God has to say in the present moment—to listen with the spirit more than with the mind.

TAIZÉ WORSHIP

The meditative style of Taizé worship is rooted in the ecumenical community of Taizé, France. Services typically include slow, repetitive singing, along with times for Scripture reading, prayer, and extended silent meditation. Candles (and sometimes icons) enhance the worship service. Many churches around the United States hold Taizé services as a way of slowing down to meditate and breathe in a corporate context.

Taizé worship lends itself to mindfulness practice in its meditative nature and the silence built into the service. The incorporation of extended repetition into song lyrics opens up room for the participant to settle into the words and practice openness to God's presence through the singing. The sights and smells of candles add to the multisensory nature of the service, inviting participants into fuller awareness of the present moment as they engage in spiritual worship.

It is perfectly normal that practitioners of any of these Christian meditative practices will experience a host of distractions during their practice, as is the case during formal mindfulness meditation practices as well. These distractions can include thoughts, feelings, sensations, and behaviors or urges. As with mindfulness meditation, the goal whenever this occurs is to escort one's attention back to a present-moment awareness, continuing on with the practice. Training in mindfulness meditation can therefore be of great benefit to Christian meditators who wish to work skillfully with distractions as they practice attentiveness to God's presence.

While we have covered only a few contemplative Christian disciplines in this section, any Christian discipline can be enhanced by applying informal mindfulness during the practice. Scripture reading, singing, corporate worship, prayer, liturgical dance, meditation, and any other devotional practice can be blended with mindful awareness. Remembering that mindfulness is intentional awareness of the present moment without judgment, what other state of mind would we want to cultivate during the practice of the spiritual disciplines besides mindful awareness? To be fully aware in the presence of God is the best place to be!

Distracted from God

Even without blending mindfulness into explicit Christian disciplines, mindfulness practice is inherently compatible with Christian spirituality. Nineteenth-century theologian Abraham Kuyper provided a framework for Christian mindfulness when he said, "No single piece of our mental world is to be hermetically sealed off from the rest, and there is not a square inch in the whole domain of our human existence over which Christ, who is Sovereign over all, does not cry: 'Mine!'"[9] When we practice mindful awareness as Christians, we do so with the fundamental belief that God's presence is everywhere and that all things are marked in some way with the creative, beautiful, and redemptive stamp of the divine.

The mindful Christian affirms that God's goodness whispers through all of creation and that we have the opportunity each day to get quiet and listen. When we practice mindfulness, we discover how many blind spots we have to truly seeing God's goodness, and we notice with some humor that this is because of a lack of sight on our part rather than a lack of revelation on God's part. Mindfulness helps us give up our need for control in our experience of God, trusting that when we are less, God is more. It shows us that when we take a step back from our mental busyness, God is ready and able to meet us in that moment.

A passage in the Gospel of Luke highlights God's love of the mindful listening posture as a method for divine connection. In the timeless story of Mary and Martha, these sisters offer a poignant example of two styles of thinking: distraction versus attentive awareness. Martha, while preparing a meal for Jesus and his disciples, was "distracted by her many tasks," while Mary "sat at the Lord's feet." Martha subsequently complained to Jesus: "Lord, do you not care that my sister has left me to do all the work by myself?" Her complaint seems fair, but Jesus surprisingly defended Mary: "Martha, Martha, you are worried and distracted by many things; there is need of only one thing. Mary has chosen the better part, which will not be taken away from her" (Luke 10:38–42).

Martha saw a problem and wanted to fix it: hungry travelers were in her home, needing to be fed, and she had the skills for the job. This problem-solving attitude is consistent with human nature. To varying degrees, people love to make things better by creating solutions and getting work done. This power of *doing* has incredible benefits for our species and for our ability to participate in God's creative work in the world. And just to be clear, Jesus loves us when we are working hard as much as when we are not. This is a relief, because there is often much hard work to be done.

But here we see Jesus call us to also carve out time to sit quietly and listen, even when it seems there is no time for it. So often, our *being*, even more than our *doing*, is what connects us to the heart of God. We see this in the response of Mary to Jesus's presence in her home. Her ability to be—to sit, to listen, to rest—creates a connection with Jesus and opens her to receive what God has to offer in that moment. Not surprisingly, this shift from *doing* to *being* is also good for our overall wellness, which is why secular mindfulness practitioners value the practice so highly.

Beyond just the activity levels in the story of Martha and Mary, this Scripture passage also highlights a needed shift in our internal state. We see Martha "worried and distracted," an internal state that plays out in her external behavior and her attitude. When she speaks, she sounds bitter, bossy, and even sarcastic with Jesus, asking him, "Do you not care?!"

I am well acquainted with the bitter Martha attitude in myself. *Why isn't anyone else willing to get this done right?* I ask during times of stress. *I guess I just have to do everything myself!* It's a biting and ungrateful attitude, one that orbits around myself rather than around my maker. And it flows from an internal sense of worry and distraction, just as it did for Martha. This is when Jesus calls out to her: "Martha, Martha, you are worried and distracted by many things; there is need of only one thing." Mary is engaged in the one thing that is needed—to sit at the Lord's feet and listen.

Because of the preponderance of scriptural passages such as this related to contemplative listening, many Christian teachers encourage the use of silence, moving from *doing* to simply *being* in God's presence as a way of connecting. But while religious upbringing has prepared many of us to cognitively understand the importance of silence, we sometimes don't know what to do with the silence other than endure it. For me, being in silence was once not much more than an act of obedience, akin to taking my spiritual medicine. Mindfulness training taught me how to use silence for cultivating a God-aware life.

Now mindful silence helps me pull away the curtain of distraction to experience God. It fosters in me the ability to dwell in God, a different goal than trying to hear a message, get a fix, or do something good for God. It gives me the opportunity to sit at Jesus's feet and saturate my senses with God's goodness. In this way, mindfulness practice has opened the eyes and ears of my heart to the richness God infuses into each moment of life, to experience God in "every square inch" of creation. Before mindfulness, I had little interest in paying attention to the present moment, because I didn't believe I would find anything there other than pain, emptiness, and boredom. Now I understand that every moment, whether pleasant or unpleasant, holds the delicious kernels of joy for which my soul longs.

Let's not dismiss the role of action in the life of a Christian; we are clearly called in Scripture to participate in the divine work of renewal. And we have lots to do. So many things in life remain unsolved, and so many of them are big and important. My young son recently asked me why people become homeless. That's a problem we haven't solved, and it's wrapped up with other problems we haven't solved as a society, including addiction and systemic racism and privilege and human behavior and the neurological impact of trauma. These things really matter, as do bullying and suicide and eating disorders and climate change, and people are hurting because we struggle to know how to fix these problems. Yes, there is much to be done as we eagerly participate in God's redemptive work.

It can take a lifetime to know when to act and when to just be—when to be Martha and when to be Mary. But learning the difference is worth a lifetime of pursuit. Learning to *be* nourishes our souls, feeds our hearts, and puts us back in the place of being a learner before our creator God. In this way, it sets us up for effective, focused, joyful service as we also *do* the things that God calls us to do.

Sacred or Secular?

This experience of *being* instead of *doing*—taking a step away from worry and distraction in order to sit and listen—can also be called mindfulness. Mindfulness can be practiced with or without an awareness of God's presence. This also is true of many other spiritual practices, such as forgiveness, love, compassion, and acts of service, as well as many other physical practices, such as daily exercise, medical treatments, and brushing our teeth regularly. With or without an active awareness of Jesus, these are all healthy practices that bring emotional, relational, and physical benefit to those who engage in them. Mindfulness is in the company of these healthy practices—both spiritual and physical—that are nearly universal in their benefit.

But although mindfulness and other healthy practices are beneficial apart from religious faith, Christians have the opportunity to acknowledge them as divine gifts through which God is at work. When Christians encounter healing and hope in the midst of mindfulness practice, they know that they have encountered Jesus. This increases the transformational power of mindfulness, not only as a generally healthy practice for the body and mind, but also as a spiritually grounded practice for the soul in pursuit of God.

So we might ask what differentiates a healthy "secular" practice from a healthy "Christian" practice? And we might answer with another question: Are there things that God is not in, places God cannot reach? In Psalm 139, the psalmist explores this same question, arriving at the unequivocal answer that God is everywhere:

> Where can I go from your spirit?
>> Or where can I flee from your presence?
> If I ascend to heaven, you are there;
>> if I make my bed in Sheol, you are there.
> If I take the wings of the morning
>> and settle at the farthest limits of the sea,
> even there your hand shall lead me,
>> and your right hand shall hold me fast.
> If I say, "Surely the darkness shall cover me,
> and the light around me become night,"
> even the darkness is not dark to you;
>> the night is as bright as the day,
>> for darkness is as light to you.

(Ps 139:7–12)

There is nowhere that God's presence is unavailable, no "secular" realm that God cannot inhabit with the sacred. God is present even in the darkness, even in death. God holds us fast, no matter our surroundings, and God sees just as clearly in the darkness as in the light.

So finding God means looking around and paying attention. In the words of Barbara Brown Taylor, finding God involves "learning to walk in the dark."[10] It means opening our eyes to the present moment, where we can be assured that God is working through all things and all circumstances, no matter how pleasant or unpleasant. It means mindful attentiveness so that our eyes can be open to divine activity.

If Christ is at work in all times and places, why do we designate some things specifically as "Christian"? Oftentimes, the word Christian is used to connote that God is being explicitly named as God. So "Christian" people are those who explicitly name Jesus Christ as God incarnate in human flesh, deserving of our devotion. "Christian" books point us toward the cultivation of a conscious relationship with God. "Christian" music identifies God as the focus of worship and tunes our hearts to notice divine presence. In all these examples, the term Christian highlights a conscious and explicit naming of divine connection, a worldview that sets God's truth at the center of all things.

In this light, what does "Christian" mindfulness look like? It is mindfulness, pure and simple, accompanied by an explicit naming of God as the source of all things observed through the practice. When we practice Christian mindfulness, we name the resulting feelings of wondering awe as worship. We point our feelings of gratitude toward our Creator. We recognize our source of peace and well-being as God. In this way, mindful Christianity brings psychological renewal that is consciously connected to God, who is actively renewing all things.

I like to think of it this way: A gift delivered from an anonymous giver will be fully enjoyed, even if the giver's identity is never revealed. However, a gift given by a loved one has double benefit, because it also enhances the relationship. Knowing the giver enriches the experience of goodness, as the heart is warmed by the connection. In this way, mindfulness is a receiving of good gifts, but Christian mindfulness is a receiving of good gifts with acknowledgment of the giver and subsequent enrichment of the divine relationship.

With this understanding, Christians can enter the practice of mindfulness with confidence, knowing that the discipline of present-moment awareness is grounded in a long tradition of Christian contemplation through the centuries. Mindfulness is one practice available for experiencing God's work and healing in the world. And when combined with Christian faith, it becomes a faith-based spiritual discipline for cultivating a connection to God's presence.

In my own life, mindfulness has become a primary pathway for cultivating worship, prayer, compassion, and divine connection. It has revitalized my faith and opened me to God's joy. The practice of Christian mindfulness can open for all of us new possibilities on the path of Christian discipleship—a path that is enriched when we become more aware of what God is up to in each moment.

Living the Practice: Mindfulness of God in the Moment

During mindfulness practice, we can turn our attention to many places, and God's presence is one of them. If you choose, set aside some time to rest your attention on God's presence as the object of your attention in the present moment. For this practice, you might set a timer for anywhere from five to twenty minutes.

Find a comfortable, upright seat, and close your eyes (or lower your gaze), bringing your attention intentionally into the present moment. Begin by noticing that you are breathing, paying attention to the physical sensations of each breath as well as sensations throughout the body. Notice the contact of your body with any surfaces (such as a chair, clothing, or air). Notice sounds that are passing through your awareness. Allow your attention to dwell with these present-moment experiences for a few moments. If it's helpful, take a couple of deep breaths, and then allow your breathing to return back to its normal rhythm.

As you breathe, acknowledge that each breath is being given by God. There's no need to think about this or analyze it. You are simply noticing that the breath is being given to you as something you receive rather than manufacture. Practice receiving each breath in the moment as it is provided by God. Spend a few minutes practicing this breath-from-God awareness.

Then gently broaden your awareness to the space where you sit. Acknowledge that God is present in the room. Again, there's no need to think about this or to feel a certain way. Just notice thoughts and feelings that arise as you attend to God's presence, but then let them go. As often as you notice your attention has wandered, bring your awareness back to God's presence in the room. Cultivate an attitude of being rather than doing as you rest in God's presence.

When your time is up, smile and thank God for being present with you during your time of quiet meditation. ◼

I am no longer involved in the measurement
of life, but in the living of it.

—*Thomas Merton*[1]

CHAPTER 4

THE METHODS OF MINDFULNESS

God's love has been poured into our hearts through
the Holy Spirit that has been given to us.

Romans 5:5

Mindfulness is both formal and informal: a set of meditation practices and a way of thinking. By practicing the former (formal mindfulness practices), we learn the latter (informal mindful awareness).

The formal approach to mindfulness—silent meditation—is like exercising at the gym or going for a run. These practices help us to strengthen our "muscle of attention" with intentionality, and they push us to stick with the mental exercise of mindfulness even when it is hard. Formal exercises might be planned into the day as part of one's routine, or they can form the basis for an extended silent retreat.

In contrast, informal mindfulness is similar to making physically healthy lifestyle choices throughout each day. These efforts are less intensive than gym workouts but equally impactful. The informal approach is less likely to be scheduled and more likely to be applied intermittently throughout each day, as often as one remembers. Informal mindful awareness can become more accessible when we are also engaging in formal mindfulness exercises. The formal practices strengthen us, laying the groundwork for the informal practice of mindfulness.

This chapter explores both formal and informal approaches to mindfulness. We will review the nuts and bolts of these practices (for those who would like to try them out) and will look at how the practices can intersect with Christian faith.

Formal Mindfulness Practices

Mindfulness-Based Stress Reduction (MBSR) functions as the basis for much of contemporary mindfulness practice in the United States.[2] This set of standardized, secular mindfulness training materials provides a rich assortment of formal mindfulness practices that are easily accessible to Christian practitioners. This section of the chapter introduces several of these formal practices, exploring their relationship to or placement within the Christian contemplative tradition. Audio guides for these MBSR mindfulness practices are widely available in digital form, helping new practitioners learn the technique, pacing, and attitude of the practices. Some suggested guides are available on my website, The Mindful Christian (www.TheMindfulChristian.com).

Most of these formal practices come with suggestions for physical postures that cultivate both alertness and relaxation during meditation. However, you are encouraged to always choose a position that is comfortable and safe for your own body. In most of the practices, you may be engaging in that particular position (or movement) for an extended period of time. So it is especially important to respect your body's natural capabilities and limits, as well as adhere to any advice from your doctor about physical constraints or medical needs. The goal in choosing a posture is to find one that best supports your practice of mindful awareness, cultivating a sense of strength, dignity, and ease in the body. If a suggested posture creates significant discomfort or interferes with attentive awareness, use intentionality in choosing a different position that is more supportive of your practice.

SITTING PRACTICE

Let's begin with the sitting practice, one of the most commonly practiced formal meditations. The sitting practice can be worked into any point of the day for any duration, with twenty minutes being a typical length. It allows space to quiet the body and mind, connect with oneself, and gain clarity.

This is a practice of stillness and openness that creates opportunity to release fruitless striving and accept all that is present in the moment. For Christians, this practice can be considered a practical application of the Scripture "Be still, and know that I am God" (Ps 46:10). In fact, some people may choose to begin their sitting practice by bringing this verse to mind, conceptualizing the experience of "knowing" God as a wordless, deep, intimate awareness that is more visceral than cognitive.

Sitting in silence slows us down for long enough to listen, putting us in a position of readiness to notice and receive whatever God has for us in that moment. Sitting practices allow us to be quiet. They allow us to take a step back from ruminative self-absorption, to create mental clarity, and to become more available to God. They move us from *thinking about* our lives into *being in* our lives, just as God made them.

Sometimes sitting practice is quite uncomfortable; some mindfulness practitioners describe consternation at their increased awareness of unpleasant feelings during practice. One mindfulness student of mine regularly experienced panic attacks in the midst of sitting practice, and she used the meditation as a way to develop a new relationship with those anxious experiences. She learned to watch the physical symptoms of anxiety come and go in her body without automatically following her escape impulse—good practice for her daily life, where that unconscious autopilot escape response had been increasing the frequency and intensity of distressing panic attacks for her throughout each day. The sitting practice gave her an opportunity to experiment with some new and more effective responses to anxious feelings.

Other times, the sitting practice comes with feelings of blissful calm, peace, and joy—a welcome opportunity to pause, breathe, and regroup in the midst of life's stress. One mindfulness student described the sitting practice as a deeply restorative exercise during a stressful season of her husband's cancer treatment. For her, the peace of the sitting practice meditation spilled over into the frequent sitting she did with her husband in waiting rooms and treatment facilities, surrounded by others who were going through similar hardships. "With all the ups and downs of my husband's health journey, these moments at the treatment facility have been rich with tranquility of mind and body," she wrote me in an email after learning the practice of mindful sitting. "Oh, that all those suffering with cancer and their family members could have this opportunity to practice mindfulness. Wow! What greater healing could take place!"

Whatever the emotional response, the sitting practice is an opportunity to pause in the midst of a day, to observe, and to connect with truths that are deeper than our passing thoughts, feelings, physical sensations, behaviors, urges, and circumstances. It is an opportunity to connect with God's provision that covers all of our needs in that moment, no matter how big or small.

How do we begin? During sitting practices, the posture is intentionally upright, alert, and dignified, with the back straight and the chest open. The practitioner takes time to settle in and become grounded, and then rests attention on the breath entering and leaving the body before expanding the awareness to other physical sensations. Attention may also be moved to thoughts, feelings, sounds, sights, or other present-moment experiences. The goal is to be intentional about wherever the attention rests throughout the practice. Each time the practitioner notices that the attention has wandered, they gently bring it back to direct observation of whatever is happening in the now.

When practicing sitting meditation, one may choose to sit on the edge of a chair or near the back of a chair with a pillow behind the back. Or one may choose to sit cross-legged at the front of a flattened meditation cushion or to kneel at the edge of a sideways meditation cushion. Whichever way you choose to sit, here are a few basic principles to keep in mind:

1. Remember to honor your body's natural capabilities and limits as you identify a posture for the sitting practice that works best for you. The following suggestions are options to be modified as needed, not rules to be followed.

2. Find a position in which your hips are above your knees and your pelvis is tilted forward.

3. Plant the feet and/or legs on the floor and the hands on the thighs. This will give you a sense of groundedness during your practice.

4. Allow the spine to straighten without being stiff, perhaps imagining a string gently pulling your head up toward the ceiling. Notice the natural curve of the spine.

5. Relax the shoulders and open the chest so that your heart is ready to receive what God has for you in that moment.

Setting up an intentional physical posture such as this during meditation practice is a way to cultivate full awareness of what is present (both mentally and physically). In this position, a Christian practitioner might imagine a sense of wholeness and strength in the body, visualizing oneself as a child of God who is loved and restored. The practitioner might also imagine the heart being opened to God during meditation practice, allowing their physical posture to reflect this openness as they rest in divine presence.

It is worth repeating that if a formal sitting meditation posture feels daunting or becomes a barrier to your practice, give yourself permission to let go of that effort. It's more important to meditate than it is to have perfect posture. We can practice mindfulness in any posture anywhere. For me, some of the most powerful moments of mindful self-care come when I'm curled up on my bed without the energy to move into a more formal position. So if you choose to meditate without an upright, alert posture, just remember to be intentional about that choice of position. We do not need to achieve anything through this practice; we are simply practicing intentionality about whatever position we choose and noticing the impact of that position on our experience in that moment.

Living the Practice: Awareness of Breath and Body

If you feel ready, look up an audio guide for mindfulness sitting practice, and follow the instructions. Or if you prefer, use the following micro-practice as a way to dip your toes in before committing to a full sitting practice.

Sit in an upright posture in a quiet place where you will not be disturbed. Then set a timer for anywhere from one to five minutes. During that time, pay attention to the sensation of breathing as much as you are able. Notice breath entering and leaving the body, and be aware of the pause that might be present at the end of each in- and outbreath. Cultivate a light and easy attention as you notice your breath. There is no need to change anything or modify the breath in any way; you are simply noticing that you are breathing, receiving with curiosity and openness each breath as it comes.

When the timer goes off, allow a gentle smile on your face. See if it is possible to bring a sense of the quiet with you into the rest of your day. ■

BODY SCAN

Another formal meditation practice is the body scan. This practice of body awareness fits well within the Christian tradition, in which there are many ways that the role of the body has been attended to, honored, and celebrated. For example, Old Testament Scripture encourages us to marvel at the wonder of our bodies as God's creation:

> It was you who formed my inward parts;
>> you knit me together in my mother's womb.

I praise you, for I am fearfully and wonderfully made.

Wonderful are your works;

that I know very well.

(Ps 139:13–14)

The New Testament adds to this veneration of the physical body by describing our bodies as temples, or locations for God's spirit to dwell: "Do you not know that your body is a temple of the Holy Spirit within you, which you have from God, and that you are not your own?" (1 Cor 6:19).

By definition, a temple is regarded as the dwelling place for deity, set aside for worship and adoration. Temples are sacred spaces that provide opportunity to absorb beauty, to wonder at creation, and to commune with God. If our bodies are truly temples, then it's wise for us to spend time honoring their service, paying attention to them. Bypassing the signals of the body is akin to running through the Sistine Chapel without stopping to look at Michelangelo's masterpiece on the ceiling or pausing to say a prayer. The body scan meditation creates opportunity to experience the body as "a temple of the Holy Spirit"—to slow down in wonder at God's magnificent creation of our physical bodies.

On a more practical level, the body scan also provides us with important information, tuning us in to our body's helpful messages. God created bodies to supply us with a constant stream of information that is incredibly useful for our day-to-day functioning. In each moment, we receive signals from the body related to comfort, safety, wellness, thoughts, feelings, and memories. Some of these signals enter conscious awareness; most do not. Research suggests that eleven billion bits of information are transmitted through our physical senses in each moment, with the eye alone transmitting ten million bits of information per second. Of all of these information bits, we are able to consciously process only fifty.[3] Our body is coursing with so much useful information that the conscious mind cannot possibly keep up. In moving the attention systematically through the entire body, the body scan practitioner develops an increased ability to be aware of helpful messages that might emerge.

The body scan practice often leads my mindfulness students to describe surprise at physical sensations of which they were unaware. Sometimes they notice they are tense and give themselves permission to relax. Sometimes they become aware of how tired they are and commit to going to bed earlier that night. One student became quite surprised at the force of air that occurred when she yawned during the practice! The body scan can also lead students to express appreciation for the functionality of their body. One student expressed deep gratitude for the calf muscles in her legs, which had been carrying her through the day without any conscious thought on her part.

How do we begin? The position we take for the body scan practice is typically lying on the back. A body scan guide might first focus on the breath, then move to the left toe, gradually up through the left leg, down to the right toe, gradually up through the right leg, through the pelvis, abdomen, chest, back, each arm (starting with the fingertips), neck, face, and head. In each of these body parts, the practitioner notices and is curious about physical sensations—perhaps temperature, tightness, tingling, blood flow, itching, contact, pressure, or other sensations that arise. Body scan guides often end with awareness of the body as a whole and then return to focus on the breath before conclusion of the practice.

Throughout this entire body scan practice, the goal is to notice sensations coming and going without judging them (negatively or positively), practicing a direct observation unfiltered by the language of thoughts. As thoughts and feelings attract attention, they are acknowledged, and attention is gently moved back to the body scan practice. When practitioners choose to follow an urge in reaction to a sensation (for example, scratching an itch or moving a limb), they do so with intentionality, noticing what they are doing with the body as they do it. This provides freedom to care well for oneself during the practice while also avoiding mindless, autopilot behaviors in response to urges.

Here are some tips for making the posture of lying on your back work for you:

1. As always, remember to honor your body's natural capabilities and limits as you identify a posture for the body scan.

2. Find a surface that is firm but comfortable, such as a yoga mat, soft rug, or firm mattress.

3. Lie on your back, keeping your spine straight, with no pillow under the head. Stretch your legs out straight, placing the heels six to eight inches apart and allowing the feet to fall naturally away from one another. You might place a pillow or rolled blanket under the knees to alleviate any discomfort in the lower back if that is helpful for you. Or you can bend the knees and lean them against one another, with feet placed hip width apart on the floor.

4. Allow your arms to rest at your sides with palms up, if that is comfortable for you.

5. Expect a possible drop in body temperature during the course of the body scan. You might consider placing a blanket over your toes or your lower body to maintain warmth.

As you progress through the body scan, be intentional about maintaining alertness. People in modern times are generally unaccustomed to being relaxed and awake at the same time; the realities of our busy lives mean that many of us are sleep deprived much of the time. If you are struggling to stay awake during the body scan, you might consider keeping your eyes partially open or taking occasional deep breaths. You can even hold one arm up at a ninety-degree angle with your elbow resting on the floor, as a falling arm is sure to wake you up if you begin drifting off. And if you feel particularly sleepy, consider the option of sitting up for the body scan, rather than lying down.

Living the Practice: Tuning In to the Body

If you feel ready, look up an audio guide for a mindfulness body scan, and follow the instructions. Or use the following micro-practice as a way to dip your toes in before committing to a full body scan practice.

Set a timer for anywhere from one to five minutes, and then use that time to tune in to physical sensations in the body. You might begin by closing your eyes and taking a deep breath. Allow your attention to turn toward the physical sensations in your body, possibly beginning with sensations such as the following:

- Contact on the skin from clothing and any surfaces that the body is touching (such as a chair or the floor)

- Air on the face

- Tightness or relaxation in the eye region, forehead, or jaw

- Warmth and coolness beneath the nose as air moves in and out, warmed by the lungs

- The diaphragm's movement up and down with the breath
- Blood moving through the body, perhaps felt as tingling or pulsing

You are likely to notice both strong and mild sensation throughout the body, as well as some regions with no sensation at all. Do your best to observe all sensations with an attitude of kindness and gentleness. There is no need to change what you find; simply be curious about sensations coming and going. As thoughts pass through the mind, notice that they are there, and then gently return your attention to physical sensations in the body. Cultivate an attitude of curiosity about what might arise, whether pleasant or unpleasant, and notice any resistance that might emerge to this mindful observation of physical sensations.

To conclude your practice, allow a gentle smile on your face and a heart whisper of gratitude to God for the wonder of the body that you have been given. ■

WALKING MEDITATION

Movement is a miracle, making it a true gift when we bring mindful attentiveness to our movements. Most of the time, most of us engage in the movement of walking with no awareness of how the body is able to propel itself through space, carefully balanced on its swaying frame. This is true of other movements as well. We blink our eyes throughout each day, rarely giving a thought to this cleansing, moisturizing movement of the eye that happens every four seconds. We lift food to our mouths without recognizing the fascinating muscle memory that allows us to hit our target almost every time.

The miraculous nature of movement is often most apparent when we lack or lose mobility. When a family acquaintance was hit by a van while riding his bike, we believed he would be paralyzed. There were cheers and tears of joy when he regained the most basic use of his legs, taking halting, wobbly steps across the hospital floor. A young friend of mine was born without the use of his legs. When he and his friends on the wheelchair basketball team speed back and forth across the basketball court making shots, I am astounded at the miracle of their movements that are so different than my own. Movement is truly miraculous, and every once in a while, we recognize that, through mindful attention.

Movement goes beyond simple body functionality. There is a connection between our physical movement and our soul movement, as the movement of our bodies expresses things that cannot be expressed with words. This is why people give more weight to our body language than our words when we speak about our emotions.[4] Whether we intend it or not, our postures and movements often tell the story of what we really feel.

Because of this body-soul connection, tuning in to our movements can be a vulnerable experience that elicits deep emotion from us. As a result, Christian worship often includes physical movements such as kneeling, lifting hands, swaying, dancing, or closing eyes. We express ourselves not only through words, but also through our physical movements.

In light of this, one of the ways to know ourselves and clear space for God's voice is to tune in to our movements. When we practice awareness of a movement like walking, we are waking up to an everyday miracle. We are cultivating wonder in how we were made, learning to appreciate what we can do. We are also stepping out of our thought stream in a very concrete way, shifting from ruminative obsession with our narratives and stories into a clearer perception of each moment, one small movement at a time.

As its name suggests, walking meditation is most often done through the movement of walking. However, any other movement can also be used as a focus for meditation. The goal of this meditation is to center attention on the physical sensations of the body moving through the air. If the focus is walking, the practitioner slows down in order to become aware of each part of each step: the lifting of the heel, the ball of the foot, the toes, the shifting of the body's weight to one side, the movement of the foot through the air, and then the placing of the heel, ball, and toes. While maintaining a light awareness of surroundings, one allows their deeper attention to come back, over and over, to the sensations of walking (or to whatever body movement to which they choose to mindfully attend).

For me, walking meditation often sparks feelings of wonder and peace, along with curiosity about the many unconscious micro-movements of muscles that are involved in keeping me balanced and upright during the course of the practice. This increases my ability to tune in to present-moment experience as I walk through the rest of my day. Walking from one place to another is a wonderful opportunity to connect with body and mind, carving out internal spaces of calm at the center of external movement.

Here are some tips for entering into a walking meditation practice:

1. As always, remember to honor your body's natural capabilities and limits as you engage in this practice of mindful movement.

2. Begin by standing still and becoming aware of physical sensations in the feet, noticing where your soles make contact with the earth below.

3. Start by shifting from side to side, observing which muscles are involved in this movement of the body.

4. Begin to walk with a deep awareness of the feet and legs moving through the air. As you progress, slow down the pace in order to become even more aware of each micro-movement, adjusting that pace to whatever best supports your attention.

5. Each time you notice that your attention has moved from your feet up to the thoughts in your head, consciously bring your attention back to the sensations of the feet moving through the air and meeting the ground.

For those practicing other types of movement meditation, these steps can be adapted to allow for slowing down and paying attention to each small component of whatever movement has been chosen.

In the process of any movement meditation, we practice mindful curiosity of other present-moment experiences that might enter the awareness (such as thoughts, feelings, sensory experiences, and behaviors or urges). We are especially cognizant of our mind's ability to pull us into stories and narratives as we go about the business of movement. We gently train our mind to come back to movement whenever we notice that our attention has been pulled again into thoughts, back into the space behind our eyes. As we move, we cultivate a sense of wonder, observing the body moving, miraculously, through space and time.

Living the Practice: Miraculous Movement

If you feel ready, locate an audio guide for a mindful walking meditation, and follow the instructions. Or use the following micro-practice as a way to dip your toes in before committing to a full movement practice.

Choose one type of movement that is available to you—perhaps walking, rocking, blinking, or stretching your arms up over your head from side to side. Set a timer for one to five minutes. During that time, rest your attention on the sensations of that particular movement. Notice shifts in muscle tension, pressure, or other physical sensations. Notice what enables the body to maintain balance as you move. Be curious about each small component of each movement, as well as the way your muscles work together. If thoughts arise during the practice—thoughts of the past or future, or perhaps judgments related to your body's natural limits or capabilities—acknowledge them and gently shift your attention back to the sensations of the body moving through space.

When the timer goes off, allow a gentle smile on your face and acknowledge the miracle of this movement in your body, no matter how big or small. ■

LOVINGKINDNESS PRACTICE

Another formal mindfulness meditation is lovingkindness practice—a meditation that centers on sending good wishes to ourselves and others. This can be a challenging practice, especially in regards to wishing well to ourselves. When left to its own devices, the mind does not tend to hang out in self-affirming, self-compassionate spaces. It can feel quite vulnerable to show ourselves kindness, as it requires us to get in touch with our personal suffering.

Showing kindness to others can be challenging as well. We want people to do the right thing and act the right way, and it is easy to strike out in judgment when that does not happen, especially if we feel wounded. So lovingkindness practice can be one of the hardest mindfulness practices of all.

When I began this practice, it was also one of the hardest mindfulness practices for me to embrace from a Christian perspective. The language of traditional lovingkindness practice initially felt like a poor fit with Christian theology. Over time, I have come to understand many ways that this practice can indeed intersect with faith and discipleship, and I experience it now as a form of prayer that blends seamlessly with Christian beliefs. We will explore lovingkindness practice here, both in its traditional mindfulness form and also in a modified, more explicitly prayerful form called a "blessing meditation."

Lovingkindness, this act of requesting good things for ourselves and others, is what we often direct toward God in Christian tradition under the label of intercessory prayer. Guides for a traditional lovingkindness practice generally follow a format such as the following:

1. Take a sitting posture that is upright and stable (see pages 59–60 for more details on the posture of sitting), and allow yourself some time to connect to your experience of body and breath in the moment.

2. Bring to mind an image of yourself—either as you are now or as you were as a small child. Direct your attention toward yourself with an attitude of kindness

and compassion. Silently repeat the following phrases (or other similar phrases) to yourself in your mind:

- May I be safe.
- May I be happy.
- May I be healthy.
- May I live with ease.

Allow a pause between each phrase, giving it time to settle into the mind and heart.

3. Bring to mind an image of someone you love or admire. Direct your attention toward that person with an attitude of kindness and compassion. Silently repeat these phrases (or other similar phrases) to yourself in your mind:

- May you be safe.
- May you be happy.
- May you be healthy.
- May you live with ease.

Repeat this process with an image of a stranger (or casual acquaintance) and again with someone who is difficult for you or who has caused you pain.

4. Bring to mind an image of all living things in the world— people, animals, and plants. Silently repeat these phrases (or other similar phrases) to yourself in your mind:

- May all beings everywhere be safe.
- May all beings everywhere be happy.
- May all beings everywhere be healthy.
- May all beings everywhere live with ease.

5. Take some time to rest in this sense of lovingkindness, paying gentle attention to your body and breath. As you conclude the practice, bring this kind attitude with you into the rest of the day, recognizing that all of us experience suffering and are in need of compassion.

My initial hesitancy about the theology of this practice centered around the requests for safety, happiness, health, and a life of ease. Doesn't Christ call us to self-sacrifice, to embrace the role of suffering in the building of our character as believers? I've heard countless sermons on God's use of discomfort to challenge us and on the need for us to step out of our comfort zones to follow God's call. I've read numerous exhortations to leave the self-focused pursuit of happiness in order to experience God's true joy. All of this made it difficult to wish safety, happiness, health, and a life on ease on myself or others when I was initially introduced to lovingkindness practice.

Because of this discomfort, my early application of lovingkindness was in the modified form of a blessing meditation, which I continue teaching to my students as an example of explicit God naming within a mindfulness practice. In the blessing meditation, we go through the same groups as described in steps 2 through 4: ourselves, a loved one, a stranger, a difficult person, and then all of God's created beings. Following the same format, we silently repeat the following prayerful phrases toward each separate group:

- May (I, you, all beings everywhere) know God's love.

- May (I, you, all beings everywhere) know God's joy.

- May (I, you, all beings everywhere) know God's rest.

- May (I, you, all beings everywhere) know God's peace.

The emphasis here is not on cognitive knowing in the mind, but the type of knowing that exists deep in the heart and the body. "Knowing" in these blessings means connecting with these truths in a way that transcends thought. This practice is one of opening up to God's blessing in our lives—to the love, joy, rest, and peace that exist in each moment. These are gifts promised to us in Scripture, gifts that are often difficult to receive in the distracted hustle and bustle of modern life.

As time has gone on, I have come to embrace the more traditional phrases of lovingkindness, when spoken in God's presence, as a natural fit with my Christian walk. The four phrases, it turns out, are things Christians often ask God for, just with different language. When spoken outside of a Christian framework, they are a psychological tool for skillfully turning our hearts toward what is good. When spoken to God, they become even more—a prayer that opens up access to the loving heart of our Creator. As we return once again to the traditional lovingkindness practice, let's break these phrases down in the context of Christian prayerfulness.

- **May we be safe.** This prayer for safety is echoed throughout Scripture as well as in modern-day expressions of Christianity. Old Testament authors repeatedly cry out to God for protection from physical harm, and New Testament authors repeatedly pray that early disciples would be protected from spiritual harm. In modern times, it is common to pray that our loved ones would be kept safe during travel, that our children would be protected from abuse or bullying, and that our ministries would have a shield of protection around them as we seek to do God's will.

  We do not expect that prayers and wishes for safety will lead to perfectly safe circumstances at all times. When sending the request for safety up to God, we know that God will remain good and steadfast even when we experience harm. We know that our suffering will be used for God's glory and for our own good. Like Jesus in the Garden of Gethsemane, we make the request along with an acknowledgment of "not my will but yours be done" (Luke 22:42). Yet we still ask, because God cares for our well-being.

- **May we be happy.** Happiness is often given a bad rap in Christian circles, with a tendency to distinguish between happiness and joy (the latter being considered more holy and desirable). This distinction can be helpful in the context of modern American materialism, where "the pursuit of happiness" has been tied to insatiable consumerism. However, I believe the problem has not been our *desire* for happiness; rather, the problem has been how far off course we have gotten in our pursuit of the goal.

True happiness is not a grabbing, fleeting, mindless numbing. It is a warm, settled, open sense of well-being that deeply permeates the soul and lights the eyes. Happiness is tied to peace, contentment, joy, positivity, hope, and gratitude. And God seems invested in cultivating this sense of happiness and well-being within us, this "fruit of the Spirit" that emerges when we settle into God's provision. Many verses in Scripture affirm this happiness, including the first psalm, where those who delight in the Lord are described as "happy . . . like trees planted by streams of water, which yield their fruit in its season" (Ps 1:1–3).

When we request happiness, we are turning toward the gift that God has for us. We are stepping out of troubled hearts and the grasping of the world, and we are rooting ourselves into the Spirit in order to live out of the well-being that God provides. None of us can feel happy all the time. But asking God for happiness is simply requesting what God is longing to give us—a sense of well-being and contentment that matches God's provision for us, that reflects our trust in God's unending care for our needs.

- **May we be healthy.** Truth be told, we all die. Therefore, asking for health in this physical body is always temporary. Sooner or later, health fails. In the meantime, Christians practice supplication for health and healing as long as God gives us breath. When my husband got pneumonia, I did not hesitate to pray for quick and complete healing. When I was laid up in bed with the flu for two weeks, I cried out to God for relief from my suffering.

  Requesting health is a way of acknowledging our frailty and God's compassion. We know that sickness is part of the fallenness in our world; sick is not how we were meant to be. This is the case for physical illness and mental illness. And we know that God grieves with us over our lack of health.

  The hallmark of Jesus's short time on earth in a physical body was to heal infirmities. He rewound the process of sickness and dying wherever he went, showing that even something as certain as death was not so certain after all. By turning the inevitability of death on its head, he gave us a glimpse of a reality bigger than death—a reality that would be showcased on a grand scale in his own physical resurrection. He showed us that even in these temporary bodies, God's care for us is profound.

  So when we request health in these temporary bodies, we proclaim our faith in God's resurrection power that will hold us through eternity. We reach out for God's healing touch as an act of worship, stating against the odds, "Lord, I believe" (John 9:38).

- **May we live with ease.** There are several versions of this lovingkindness phrase, including "May we be free from suffering" and "May we be peaceful and strong." At the core is a request to move from unproductive striving into peaceful acceptance. There are so many ways we push and pull, lift and heave, force and hammer and jerk on life. Many of these efforts do not get us what we want.

  Mindfulness teaches us to notice when our striving is helpful and when it is not, when we have the option to live with more ease. Jesus urges us toward this life of greater ease when he says, "Come to me, all you that are weary and are carrying heavy burdens, and I will give you rest. Take my yoke upon you, and learn from me; for I am gentle and humble in heart, and you will find rest for your souls. For my yoke is easy, and my burden is light" (Matt 11:28–30).

  Trying harder is not the way of Christ. Receiving God's forgiveness and grace is the Christian way. Trying harder is the way of the older brother in the parable of the prodigal son. Returning to God as Father and finding acceptance is the way of the younger son, the one who found rest in his father's work rather than his own.[5] So when we pray for "ease," we are inviting a life of openness to God's work. We are making a choice to trust God's work above our own striving. We are opening up to the river of goodness running through our souls, no matter what challenges we face in our lives. And we are affirming that God is good and therefore we can rest, safe in our Father's arms, knowing that he's got this.

You may have noticed that lovingkindness and blessing meditations include wishing well to the difficult people in our lives. In doing so, these practices take on one of Christ's biggest challenges, found in the Sermon on the Mount: "Love your enemies and pray for those who persecute you" (Matt 5:44). When we wish well to those who are difficult for us, we are practicing forgiveness and love for our enemies. We are living out the high standard that God calls us to: loving those who have hurt us. This is not equivalent to being in ongoing relationship with our enemies. Whether or not to maintain those relationships is a separate question from the act of forgiveness. But it is an attitude of lovingkindness that puts us on equal moral footing with our enemies, recognizing that "there is no one who is righteous, not even one. . . . All have sinned and fall short" (Rom 3:10, 23).

At its most fundamental level, lovingkindness practice is the cultivation of a compassionate stance toward ourselves and others. It is living into the truth that God created this world and called it good from the very beginning (Gen 1:31), and that his ongoing love for the world was expressed through his own incarnation as one of us (John 3:16). It is a practice of receiving the gift of compassion that God offers us each day, and passing that compassion on to others in fulfillment of our Christian calling to love one another (John 13:34–35). By compassionately extending God's compassion to others, we are holding them in God's presence and asking for good things in their lives.

Living the Practice: Extending Blessing

If you feel ready, locate an audio guide for a lovingkindness meditation, and follow the instructions. Or use the following micro-practice as a way to dip your toes in before committing to a full lovingkindness practice.

Chose a quiet place where you will not be disturbed, as well as a physical posture that supports your attention. Identify someone in your mind whom you love, admire, and/or respect—someone who brings up positive feelings when you think of them. This could be someone you know well or someone you have never met. Then set a timer for anywhere from one to five minutes and begin by focusing in on the physical sensations of breathing.

As you settle into this breath awareness, extend a silent blessing to the person you have identified that you love or admire. Notice them as a cotraveler on life's journey, as someone created by God. Notice how the truest thing about them is that, like you, they are dearly loved and they reflect God's image. In God's presence, wish them well in your heart and express gratitude to God for making them just as they are. Extend a prayer for safety, happiness, health, and ease in their life. Then extend the same prayer for yourself before bringing your brief meditation to a close and continuing on with your day. ■

RAISIN MEDITATION

God made the human body to be fueled by food—and also made much of our food to taste quite delicious. However, people often approach the act of eating as a mindless, rushed task to check off the list. The raisin meditation is a formal mindfulness practice that helps us slow down while we eat, appreciating our food and our bodies while reducing overall stress and increasing a sense of connection to the rest of the world.

Unlike the previous practices, the raisin meditation does not come with guidelines for a particular posture. All that is needed is a raisin and a place where you will not be interrupted for approximately fifteen minutes. (If you choose, you can substitute another raw or minimally processed food for the raisin in this eating practice.) Here are some steps to follow:

1. Place one raisin in your hand. Pretend that you have never seen this object before and that you know nothing about it. Get curious about your observations.

2. Beginning with the sense of sight, explore variations in color, shape, lightness, darkness, and any other visual features of the object.

3. Acknowledging now that this is a raisin, take a moment to consider the journey that it has been on in order to reach you. It emerged on a vine as a baby grape, received sun and rain, and grew into a mature fruit. It was harvested, dried, packaged, transported, shelved, and purchased. All along the journey, numerous people contributed their time and energy in order to bring this raisin to you. This tiny piece of fruit demonstrates our deep interconnectedness with one another and with the earth.

4. Pause to notice any thoughts you might be having during this raisin meditation, whether pleasant or unpleasant. Perhaps you have expectations about whether or not you will enjoy eating the raisin, or you may have judgments (positive or negative) about the meditation itself. Perhaps your thoughts have wandered into remembering or planning. Whatever your thoughts, acknowledge them without judgment, and then bring your attention back to the raisin in your hand.

5. Now lift the raisin to your ear. With just a slight amount of pressure, roll it gently between your forefinger and

thumb, and listen, noticing whether you are able to detect a faint crackling sound.

6. Move the raisin beneath your nose. (Notice how your arm and hand know just how to do this.) Use your sense of smell to experience the raisin. Notice any reaction in your body to the aroma—perhaps saliva in the mouth or a shifting sensation in the stomach. Notice any emotional response associated with the smell of the raisin.

7. Move the raisin to your lips, and then set it on your tongue. Without chewing, roll the raisin on your tongue and explore texture. Notice reactions in the mouth and body.

8. Form the intention to take a bite, and then take one bite. Notice any waves of taste emanating from the raisin, and how the taste and texture change in the mouth. Notice any urge to swallow.

9. Form the intention to chew, and then slowly chew the raisin. Observe changing textures and tastes in the mouth, physical responses in the body, and urges to swallow.

10. Form the intention to swallow, and then swallow the raisin. Notice as it moves down the throat into the stomach, and the way that the tongue and mouth move to finalize the eating of the raisin. Notice that your body is now exactly one raisin heavier.

This is a very different way of eating than our typical approach, which tends to include minimal awareness as we push through each bite, on autopilot. Because of this, eating practices such as the raisin meditation can have surprising results. One of my students was flooded with love for her raisin in the course of a raisin meditation, barely able to contain the strong feelings of affection that arose toward her raisin. Others have described surprise at the unexpected thoughts that pop up in connection with their raisin (for example, a memory of grandmother) or curiosity about the previously undetected physical responses that occur while eating the raisin (such as an almost irresistible urge to swallow). And it is not uncommon that practitioners of mindful eating discover surprises in their food preferences, once they start paying attention. Mindful eating has both enhanced and reduced the pleasure of certain foods for anyone who has engaged in this practice.

Mindful eating is an example of many "ordinary" activities that can be enhanced through mindful awareness. Bringing this type of attentiveness to exercise, touch, household chores, personal hygiene, sex, work, music, or conversation can transform our ability to enjoy and skillfully engage in those activities. When we pay more attention to our daily activities of life, we find all kinds of surprises and signals that can enhance our joy and give us helpful information along the way.

Living the Practice: Mindful Drinking

If you feel ready, follow the written instructions for engaging in a raisin meditation. Or you can use the following micro-practice as a way to dip your toes in before committing to a full eating practice.

Choose a drink to use for a short mindful-drinking practice. This might be a glass of ice water, a cup of warm tea, or any other potable liquid.

For approximately one minute, use all of your senses to mindfully engage with and experience this drink. Notice what you see when you look at it—colors, shapes, reflections, and so on. Notice what you hear when you listen to it. Notice the taste and the smell of the drink. Notice the physical sensations of holding the drink in your hand, as well as the physical sensations in your body (including your mouth and throat) as you drink it.

For all of these senses, see if it's possible to have the direct experience outside the filter of thought and language. Also, pay attention to any reactions in your body, thoughts, or emotions throughout the exercise.

When you are ready, return to your more typical pace of drinking, with the option to work this type of curious awareness into the rest of your eating and drinking experiences through the rest of the day, if you choose. ■

BREATHING SPACE

The formal meditation practices we have explored so far tend to be practiced in periods of ten to sixty minutes per sitting. Over time, mindfulness practitioners gain the ability to "drop in" to the present moment more quickly—to connect with a sense of deep peace or calm on the go.

Our final formal mindfulness practice for this chapter, the breathing space, is simply that: a one- to three-minute period of silence used to breathe, reconnect with the present moment, and check in with how we are doing. This can be done in any place where you have the freedom to close your eyes, sit up straight, and be uninterrupted for a short period. The position of a breathing space is generally consistent with that of a longer sitting practice, just with a shortened application.

Any method of spiritual discipline or self-care requires both short and long strategies. We learn the long and hard practices that stretch us and mold us. We also learn the short practices that keep us healthy throughout the day and help to get us through crisis points. Both the short and long strategies shape us and strengthen our ability to hear God's voice and be well.

One mindfulness practitioner I know uses the breathing space on a regular basis when she turns off her car. Taking one minute simply to breathe and check in gives her the needed presence of mind to smoothly transition to the next place or activity of her day. The breathing space serves as a calming and grounding practice for her, adding moments of ease in the midst of a busy schedule. It is a brief and simple act of self-care.

There are a variety of ways to approach the breathing space practice, and many different guides are available. Here's one approach that uses the metaphor of an hourglass shape to describe your awareness through the practice:

1. Find a comfortable position that supports your attention.

2. Set a timer to ring in three minutes. Then close your eyes, if you choose.

3. Begin with a broad awareness of how you are doing; this wide span of awareness is the top of the hourglass. Notice thoughts, feelings, and physical sensations. "Drop in" to the body, becoming aware of what is present for you right now. Allow your awareness to remain in this wide space of exploration for approximately one minute. (There's no need to watch the clock, as these times are only estimates.)

4. Now shift your awareness, narrowing your attention to the breath. This is the middle of the hourglass. Notice the sensations of the breath entering and leaving the body. Notice where you feel the breath most vividly—perhaps at the tip of the nose or in the chest, or perhaps somewhere else. Allow your attention to rest here on the breath for approximately one minute.

5. Shift your awareness one more time, broadening your attention once again, this time feeling the whole body breathing as you widen your focus at the bottom of the hourglass. Notice the sensations of the air entering through the nose, filling the chest, and filling the whole body from head to toe. Notice the sensations of the air leaving as the body empties out once again. Be in tune with the entire body breathing all on its own, without any effort needed on your part. Rest your awareness here for approximately one minute, until the bell rings.

As an alternative to this hourglass structure, you can also use the entire time to simply focus on the body or breath, or you can allow yourself to bypass any specific focus and just notice whatever is happening during that time. However you choose to structure your breathing space, it can be used either as a scheduled time or simply inserted into the natural pauses of your day (as described in the next Living the Practice exercise).

Whatever your technique or timing, approach this brief practice with an attitude of gentleness and care toward yourself. It is a radical act of self-care in the midst of life's many challenges— an opportunity to step out of the thought stream briefly and open your heart to God's rest and goodness. Even one minute of breathing can make all the difference in the world, enabling you to move through your day with increased calm, joy, and connection.

Living the Practice: Space to Breathe

If you feel ready, locate an audio guide for a breathing space meditation, and follow the instructions. Or you can use the method described in the following paragraphs as a way to dip your toes in before committing to a full breathing space practice.

Choose one situational cue to use today as the prompt for a short breathing space. This might be the moments when you turn off your car (before opening the door to exit), sit down at your desk (before opening up email), or press start on the coffee pot (before moving on to the next thing)—anything that you expect to do one or more times each day.

Each time you arrive in that situation, use it as a cue to take three deep breaths. Briefly tune in to your body, and take notice of any thoughts of feelings that are present.

Then proceed with your day, bringing with you an increased awareness of your breath and body as you move into your next activity. ∎

Informal Mindful Awareness

We have explored several formal mindfulness meditations, all of which involve pausing to be silent and engage in a structured observation of our experience. Informal mindfulness is less structured and more fluid, and it builds on all of these formal practices. Thus, it requires many fewer pages to describe!

In all areas of wellness—physical, mental, and spiritual—there are numerous small decisions we make throughout each day that move the tide of our overall wellness in one direction or another.

Informal mindfulness practice is a way of keeping the tide flowing in the direction of increased wellness by paying attention to the present moment throughout each day, whenever we remember to do so. While formal practices require silent periods of dedicated practice, informal practice occurs as often as we remember to apply the attitude of mindfulness during the course of each day.

Any intentional moment of mindful, curious, open, nonjudgmental awareness during the course of a day can be considered informal mindfulness. This could look like pausing to feel the bottoms of your feet, to examine an insect, or to give yourself a kind word. Whatever the focus of attention, informal mindfulness practice involves returning to present-moment experience whenever we notice that our mind has wandered into the past or future. It involves a focus on physical sensations, creating observational distance from thoughts and feelings as we shift awareness from the mind into the body on a regular basis. It involves letting go of our experiences throughout the day as passing phenomena rather than holding on to them as identity markers. It involves a cultivation of curiosity and kindness toward ourselves and others.

For years, I tried applying mindfulness principles informally to my life—watching the coffee drip, noticing the greenness of the grass, experiencing the tactile sensations of various objects—without any success. At the time, these principles were unhelpful because I had not yet engaged in formal mindfulness meditation practices. It was important for me to begin with the hard work of formal mindfulness practices before I could develop the skills of informal mindfulness and experience the benefits.

As one engages in formal mindfulness practices, informal mindfulness becomes increasingly available throughout each day. In any moment, we can choose to pause and turn toward our experience with curiosity. While informal practice has no required structure, one might ask oneself questions during this pause:

- What thoughts are in my mind?

- What emotions are present?

- What behaviors am I showing, or what urges do I have?

- What physical sensations (such as contact, pressure, tension, ease, heartbeat, breath) do I feel? What do I hear, see, smell, or taste?

When asking these simple questions, we turn toward our experience with an attitude of self-compassion, perhaps even smiling at ourselves and our experience in that moment. Whatever is happening, whoever we are with, whatever we are feeling, we tell ourselves, "I'm okay. Let me see what's going on with me right now." And we extend this same compassion toward others, nurturing an attitude of compassion and kindness toward all whom God loves. This blend of compassion toward self and others softens and soothes our hearts, putting us in touch with the transformative power of God's love. Something within me heals and is made whole when I look out the bus window and extend blessing to each house, when I walk down the street and silently wish well on the passersby, when I look with grateful kindness on a tree or a pet or a person I don't know, glad that they exist. Looking on others with lovingkindness orients my heart to love, care about, and empathize with them. It moves me out of myself, while simultaneously including myself in the circle of compassion that I mindfully extend to others. It reduces my irritability with the world, helping me to be more understanding of us all as we struggle through this life together.

Informal mindfulness practice such as this clears the way for the Christian to see through the clutter and gain an awareness of God's presence throughout the day. Waking up to what is going on in each moment leads to clearing of unconscious mental distractions and obtaining clarity about what is happening in the moment. At the foundation of what is going on in the moment is God—always present, always at work, always available, whether or not we notice. Informal mindfulness is an invitation to step out of self-centered orbit and connect with God's work in the moment.

Mindfulness is learning to be at home exactly as we are, exactly where we are, in the deepest part of ourselves. Informal mindfulness can be described as walking and maintaining the internal path to that home center on a regular basis, walking through the jungle of internal and external experiences whenever we choose in the course of a day. The path to our home center has been established through the use of formal mindfulness practices, and then we use informal mindfulness to maintain it. This takes us deeper than our surface-level reactions, opening up new possibilities for spiritual growth, worship, and prayer throughout each day.

All mindfulness practices, both formal and informal, cultivate an understanding that God is providing all that is needed in each moment. God waits to lead us through the muddle of our thoughts and feelings, through uncomfortable physical sensations, through the blinding fog of life. When we pause to pay attention, God leads us back to that still place deep within that is home, a quiet place that we carry within us every day in every moment. Through mindfulness practice, we follow God's lead in the midst of a chaotic world and repeatedly reconnect with peace, quiet, and well-being at our core. We find our way home.

Being Mindful, Not Flooded

We've reviewed a variety of formal mindfulness meditation practices in this chapter and explored the practice of informal mindful awareness as well. We pause here to look at the importance of monitoring our individual responses while learning the practice.

Every healthy practice has associated risks and limitations. For example, despite the well-established benefits of physical exercise, every year many patients visit emergency rooms with injuries related to sports and physical activity. [6] Furthermore, individual benefits of physical exercise vary based on a wide range of factors, such as age, sex, and health status.[7] These qualifiers also are true for healthy mental practices, including mindfulness meditation. Not everyone responds in exactly the same way. In fact, a small percentage of new meditation practitioners report negative side effects from the practice, such as increased anxiety, depression, or exacerbation of other psychological conditions. Distressing thoughts or feelings individuals had been previously suppressing or even repressing can emerge, and meditation practitioners may be unsure how to manage these surprising experiences on their own. Also, some practitioners may experience no significant effects at all, positive or negative.[8]

Research has not yet provided clear indicators of which variables predict these different outcomes from mindfulness meditation. However, individuals may be at particular risk for unpleasant reactions if they have a recent history of major depressive episodes, suicide attempts, substance misuse, or trauma, especially if they have not previously worked through these issues in treatment. Given that all of these experiences can involve a history of emotional numbing as a natural coping mechanism, entering into formal mindful meditation may feel emotionally flooding and overwhelming. Practitioners vulnerable to dissociation (such as those with self-harming tendencies or significant trauma history) may struggle to remain grounded in the practice or may have limited capacity for the observational distance needed to moderate painful thoughts and feelings.

Individuals may also be at higher risk for dissatisfaction with outcomes if they expect mindfulness to produce calmness, relaxation, or thought clearing. The reality is that mindfulness practitioners sometimes experience increased distress before deeper healing can occur, particularly during formal practices. (As the saying goes, "You can't heal what you can't feel.") This can be confusing and challenging for those with intense psychological responses. But any positive effects of mindfulness are gained by learning a new relationship with distressing thoughts and feelings rather than avoiding them—by developing the capacity to observe experiences without mindless engagement and learning to shift the attention between experiences as needed with intentionality and self-compassion.

While many individuals benefit from learning mindfulness practices on their own, skilled coaching (such as completion of a Mindfulness-Based Stress Reduction course) can be quite helpful for learning the techniques. For individuals with any of the risk factors listed previously, it is strongly recommended that you take an extra step and ensure professional mental health support (along with a robust system of other supports) as you learn the practice of mindfulness meditation. This will help in customizing the practice to your individual needs, thereby reducing the risk of unpleasant responses and supporting maximum benefit from the practice.

For all practitioners of mindfulness meditation, it is advisable to refrain from forcing oneself into any practices that feel highly triggering. The goal of mindfulness is not to follow every instruction that is given, nor is it to follow the whim of wherever our mind wants to take us. Instead, the goal is to notice what we are doing with our mind when we are doing it—to be intentional about where we put our mind, our awareness. So if you notice that a particular focus of attention feels emotionally flooding, give yourself permission to move your attention to another focal point for as long as you need.

A good modifier for every meditation instruction is "if you choose." The attitude of self-compassion (explored in more depth in chapter 8) serves as a guide for discerning when to lean in or lean out as uncomfortable thoughts and feelings arise. Practitioners can utilize the power of mindful, self-compassionate attention to notice when and how the practice of mindfulness is most helpful for them as individuals.

Having explored a host of technicalities in this chapter, let's end with a simple practice that brings us back to the emotional center of mindfulness within a Christian framework: the invitation to cultivate that sacred space of "home" provided by God deep within each of us. Take a breath with me, if you choose, and let's take some time to explore the experience of home with the following practice.

Living the Practice: Learning the Pathway Home

What feels like home for you? Is it a house? Or a person? A certain neck of the woods or a favorite song? Is it a treasured wall hanging, a familiar meal, or a worn-out sweatshirt? Is it a particular memory or place that ignites peace in your soul?

When you're sad, frightened, or displaced, what do you go to in order to get back in touch with yourself? What grounds you? What is home?

As you arrive at your image of home, sit in silence for a few moments, and allow yourself to savor that sense. Allow yourself to go there completely in your mind, as if you were really in that place.

- Observe each of your senses there: What do you see, feel, hear, smell, and taste?
- What emotion is present for you?
- What do you notice in your body? Where does that sense of home reside inside of you?

Notice the physical and emotional impact of being "home." Notice that this feeling is inside of you, and that it is a place you can return to over and over. Notice that God is in that sacred space of home, and thank God for providing in this way.

This practice might be challenging for you, and it may be hard to find a sense of home. That's okay—no worries. With mindfulness practices, we are not trying to manufacture something that is not there, and we are not trying to feel any differently. So if you find worry or anger or sadness in the place of "home," that's what to feel. Your sense of home will emerge over time as you spend time with whatever is there. Be kind, be gentle, be patient with yourself as you keep your eye out for the pathway home. ■

Earth's crammed with Heaven,
And every common bush afire with God;
But only he who sees, takes off his shoes.

—*Emily Barrett Browning*[1]

CHAPTER 5

WHAT'S IN A MOMENT?

This is the day that the Lord has made;
let us rejoice and be glad in it.
Psalm 118:24

In each moment, many, many things are going on. We are constantly experiencing innumerable thoughts, feelings, physical sensations, behaviors, and urges. And God is always present, up to something new. If you think of each of these present-moment experiences as one colored bead and then imagine dumping all of the colored beads sold at your local craft store into one large bin, this provides a picture of the multifaceted, complex, varied experiences that are blended together for us in each moment. Altogether, it's a lot to sort through, and most of our experiences go unnoticed as a result.

   You might think of mindfulness as going up to that large bin of mixed-up multicolored beads and pulling out one at a time for examination. One color of bead is a thought, such as "I don't know what to make for dinner." Another is a feeling, such as anxiety. Another is a physical sensation, such as tension in the jaw. Another is a behavior, such as bouncing your knee. Another is an urge, such as the desire to open your phone and search the web for a recipe. Another is God's presence, which is with you at that moment.

Mindfulness allows us to take time to differentiate our experiences in this way, examining them with curiosity as separate elements. This gives us a more detailed and accurate understanding of what is present for us in that moment, as compared with the blur of experience that typifies most of our waking moments. When we pay attention in this detailed fashion, we expand our awareness to include experiences we hadn't noticed before, increasing connection with ourselves, our environment, and also our creator God.

The goal of this observation is not to change what is there. We are simply putting a little distance between our conscious mind and our experience, creating some space to observe and become more aware. Whether or not we like what we find, we approach the moment with openness, curiosity, and acceptance, and without judgment. This attentive awareness is healing, in and of itself.

And then we watch as our experience changes, all on its own. We observe the coming and going of our experiences as if we are watching leaves floating down a stream, knowing that they always move on. This changing landscape of experience is sometimes pleasant and sometimes unpleasant, but it is always an adventure when we truly pay attention.

Given all of the different elements that make up a moment— all of the colors of beads—we'll take some time now to identify some of the areas where one might focus attention during mindful awareness, beginning with thoughts.

Thoughts

The brain generates a constant stream of thoughts, most of which fall outside conscious awareness. There are some thoughts of which we are very aware, which may cause distress or joy. But most of our thoughts zip around the brain without our noticing, and many of them are wreaking havoc in the process. Occasionally, being lost in thought is a pleasant experience. Often, it is not.

Thoughts are quite varied in their type. Some are about the past, and others are about the future, with some occasionally about the present. We have thoughts that are opinions, judgments, and predictions. We have thoughts that are spiritual, factual, curious, worried, hopeful, or imaginative. Some of our thoughts are ones we like; others, not so much. For most of us, our many thoughts center on ourselves and what others think about us. Sometimes we have thoughts about others' well-being.

Most thoughts have an emotional tenor, whether pleasant, unpleasant, or neutral, but with mindful awareness, we separate out thoughts from feelings. We notice the content of our thoughts with objective curiosity while acknowledging the accompanying emotion. We observe our thoughts as brain activity more than truth, noticing that thoughts are not facts. When we notice our thoughts in this attentive way, we avoid being swept away by them, mindlessly unaware.

NEURAL NETWORKS

The benefit of observing thoughts mindfully can be explained partially by brain science. Neuroscientists have identified in the brain multiple neural networks that are involved in executive control and attention,[2] and the balance of activity in these networks has a profound impact on the emotional experience of being human. One of the networks particularly relevant to mindfulness is the default mode network (DMN).[3] The DMN is a daydreamer. This neural network pulls us into a resting, introspective mode with no particular area of focus. When the DMN is active, we are lost in internal stimuli without a sense of connection to the external world. Examples of this include getting lost in our favorite piece of music, daydreaming about an upcoming beach vacation, or mentally replaying a painful comment made about us by a coworker.

The DMN supports important mental functions such as autobiographical memory, moral reasoning, and theory of mind, so it plays a crucial role in our ability to thrive. However, when we become stuck in internal rumination with limited engagement in focused attention, this can cause problems. Research shows that overactivation of the DMN is correlated with depression, anxiety,[4] and inattentiveness (including attention-deficit/hyperactivity disorder, or ADHD),[5] and this shows up in brain scans of individuals with these conditions. Being lost for too long in wandering, unfocused states of attention can increase our propensity toward painful emotions.

One way to deactivate the DMN is to engage in cognitively demanding tasks, including mindfulness meditation. When we meditate, we step out of wandering attention states and activate another neural network, that of the central executive network (CEN). The CEN is a problem solver that helps us to stabilize and move forward skillfully during times of challenge, and it inhibits the rumination of the DMN.

As we practice mindfulness meditation, we enhance our ability to inhibit the DMN as needed by activating the CEN: we deactivate self-referential, negatively biased thoughts and activate stabilizing, problem-solving thoughts. This decreases our vulnerability to painful emotional states. In this way, the effectiveness of mindfulness has a biological basis in the brain's neural pathways. Practicing mindfulness supports neurological health and helps us live into all that God made us to be.

JUDGMENTAL THOUGHTS

When practicing mindful observation of thoughts, there is one type of thinking we pay particular attention to: judgments. Because mindfulness involves the practice of a nonjudgmental attitude, it is especially helpful to be aware of judgmental thoughts, whether the judgments are negative, positive, or neutral.

Recently, I had a conversation with a friend about getting older and our changing perception of birthdays. We talked about how we shifted from seeing a birthday as a day of celebration to seeing it as an ominous marker replete with meaning. On my twentieth birthday, I thought, "This is fun! I'm two decades old!" On my forty-fourth birthday, I thought, "This is crazy! I've done nothing worthwhile with my life, and I'm turning into an old lady."

Our days are filled with these types of interpretations and assignments of meaning that have no factual connection to reality. While a birthday is a day just like any other, we are quick to use it as a basis for comparison to others and interpretation of our success in life. We play similar mental gymnastics on every other day of the year, greeting each moment like an investigative reporter who must know who, what, why, when, and where. There is rarely a moment that can just be, without a stream of scrutiny or analysis. And the judgment we place on each moment takes a toll on us.

This human tendency can be very helpful in some situations (when conducting investigative reporting, for example). But when this type of "grilling" is applied to each emotion and everyday life experience, it becomes a breeding ground for emotional pain. In the mindfulness tradition, we speak of this as one of the ways that the mind creates its own suffering.

When I first began the practice of mindfulness, I was shocked to realize the quantity of judgmental thoughts coursing through my mind in every moment. What had previously seemed like simple— and true—observations of reality turned out to be unnecessary indictments of my experience. These judgments were directed toward my environment, myself, and my fellow humans. It did not take me long to discover that my self-critic had gotten carried away.

The damaging role of judgmental criticism has been researched by the Gottman Institute. Through their research with couples, John and Julie Gottman have identified four predictors of relational doom: criticism, contempt, defensiveness, and stonewalling. When any of these behaviors dominates a couple's communication style, it spells danger. Because of the accuracy with which these behaviors predict divorce, the Gottmans call them "the four horsemen of the apocalypse."[6]

These horsemen not only damage our romantic relationships, they damage all of our relationships, including the relationship with ourselves. Criticism, contempt, defensiveness, and stonewalling toward ourselves are deeply damaging to our well-being. When we intentionally take a nonjudgmental stance in mindfulness, we are modifying our tendency toward these behaviors of the four horsemen, in relationship to others and to ourselves. Mindful, nonjudgmental curiosity helps the four horsemen to recede.

Letting go of judgment does not mean abandonment of wise discernment. There are times and places to name evil and to call out injustice, and God requires us to stand up for what is right. But God is the ultimate judge, not us. And when we call out injustice, we want to do it effectively. We want to make our words and actions count. We want to choose the right battles and make the right truces.

A mindful, nonjudgmental stance cultivates the presence of mind needed for sound judgment and action. It allows us to remain with our direct experience long enough to gather and absorb needed information before reacting. Without this nonjudgmental pause, there is greater risk that our good efforts will inadvertently perpetuate toxic cycles or even harm others. Perhaps we try to show we are embracing of all people but in the process convey a patronizing or superior attitude toward those we are trying to embrace. Perhaps we extend help to those in need but in the process support dependency and devalue competencies. Perhaps we proclaim truth and justice to the world but in the process use a tone that is alienating and turns people away from God. We are all guilty of intending good and yet doing harm when we operate on autopilot.

Not only does the nonjudgmental stance increase effective action, it also decreases the painful emotional triggers of our judgmental thoughts. Judgments of others tend to spark feelings of anger. Judgments of ourselves tend to spark feelings of depression. This flow between judgmental thoughts and uncomfortable emotions proceeds largely undetected when we are not practicing mindful awareness. One small thought flickering through the mind triggers a flood of thoughts behind, and it takes almost no time at all for us to become completely lost in that flood of thoughts.[7] Practicing nonjudgment helps us to slow that process down, providing us with options for decreasing unconscious triggers.

Feelings

One of the tricks in a therapist's tool bag is helping clients differentiate between thoughts and feelings. When a client says, "I just feel like this is too much," the astute therapist might respond, "You are *thinking* this is too much. But what is your emotion or feeling?" The client may, for example, be feeling afraid or hopeless or angry. Helping clients differentiate between the two provides opportunity to identify thoughts and feelings as distinct elements of their experience, with awareness of how the two are affecting one another.

Mindfulness provides opportunity to notice feelings as separate from thoughts in this way and then to respond to those feelings with care. We become present to feelings with kind, open, gentle, curious attentiveness, experiencing them directly and outside the filter of thoughts. This reduces the likelihood that we will be controlled or overwhelmed by our feelings.

There is a temptation to view unpleasant feelings as problems to be fixed or changed, to react with judgmental thoughts such as "I shouldn't feel this way." And there is also a temptation to cling to pleasant feelings, wanting them to last forever. But with mindful awareness, we choose not to label feelings as good or bad, and we recognize that they are passing phenomena that will change on their own. We lean directly into our feelings, whether pleasant or unpleasant, accepting them as part of our experience in that moment, without judgment.

In a cultural climate that idolizes happiness, mindful awareness of unpleasant feelings can be especially challenging; the feelings can catch us off guard and be perceived as threats or evidence of personal failure. When we have unhappy feelings, we might wonder if it is our fault, if people are judging us negatively, or if we are burdening others. These types of judgmental thoughts can trigger and retrigger our uncomfortable emotions. The accepting stance of mindfulness provides a less triggering, less painful path for navigating feelings as we disengage from the struggle and watch them change over time.

Susceptibility to unpleasant feelings can be especially high in certain seasons and settings. Let's take Christmas, for example. This holiday comes with lots of expectations: twinkling lights, happy families, delicious food. But I rarely have the perfect Christmas experience. Without mindfulness, I am prone to negatively judge my malfunctioning Christmas tree lights, the lack of carols, and the difficult family dynamics. They don't match up with my expectations, and this leads to unpleasant feelings. But with mindfulness, I recognize these experiences (including my feelings) as part of the normal fluctuations of life, and I observe them with open curiosity. Mindfulness helps me release expectations, expect ups and downs, and even welcome them as part of life's grand adventure.

With mindful awareness, we notice that in a world of trouble, our feelings are always shifting and changing but that at a deeper level, we are okay through it all. And isn't this what Jesus asked of us as he neared the end of his own difficult, earthly life? "In me you may have peace. In this world, you will have trouble. But take heart! I have overcome the world" (John 16:33). This is a beautiful summary of the nonjudgmental attitude of mindfulness toward "trouble," including emotional trouble. We can (and will) have trouble yet still have peace. We can (and will) experience grief, disappointment, anger, and fear yet still have peace. We can (and will) find that the world is a broken mess yet still experience beauty and joy amidst it all. This is mindfulness. This is also Christian faith.

So mindful Christianity brings this attitude of radical acceptance toward our feelings, even when they are troubled. We practice accepting all feelings just as they are, recognizing that God is with us right here in the midst of it all.

GOD'S FEELINGS

Have you ever read Scripture with an eye to understanding God's emotions? Have you noticed how intense they are? Emotions, even the uncomfortable ones, are part of the divine image. When we have feelings, pleasant or unpleasant, we are reflecting God; we are showing a part of what God looks like.

Old Testament writers had a raw and personal view of God's affective landscape. They did not view God's emotions as problematic or bad. Through their emotionally attuned cultural lens, they saw that God is sometimes filled with anger and rage and frustration. God is sometimes jealous and heartbroken when the people stray. God has periods of rejoicing and feelings of love and tenderness. The Old Testament writers never try to hide or suggest that God tries to hide this wide range of emotions; instead of dismissing or demonstrating shame about God's emotions, the writers simply record them.

In the New Testament, we continue to see God displaying a wide range of emotions, this time in the human form of Jesus. Jesus lamented Jerusalem's rejection of God, which he knew would lead to the destruction of the city. He angrily knocked over tables of money changers in the temple because his Father's house was being desecrated. He wept over the death of his friend Lazarus, even when he knew the "rational" reality that Lazarus would soon be raised to life.

This story of Lazarus's resurrection (John 11:1–44) demonstrates Jesus's relationship with emotions and our own human tendency to resist healing work in our lives because we can't see beyond our own feelings. Martha and Mary are again the main characters of this story. Attached to their painful emotions, they accused Jesus of showing up too late after the death of their brother Lazarus. When he promised resurrection, they couldn't see that he meant in the present moment. When he said, "Take away the stone," they got tripped up over the practicalities and argued that it would smell too bad.

In the midst of painful emotion, resistance is often our own first response to the hope of resurrection. Yet Jesus persists with us until we see and receive resurrection as the gift that it is. At the same time, God feels the pain with us. In the story of Lazarus, Jesus entered into the darkness with Mary and wept right along with her. His weeping was not a rational act; he knew that Lazarus would soon be alive again. Instead, his weeping was a participation in the grief of Mary and her friends, a sharing in their communal experience of grief. Jesus willingly mirrored their emotional experience, much as we do for one another. Sharing each other's emotional pain is a great gift during times of struggle.

Once resurrection happens, it takes ongoing intentionality to stay open, rather than resistant, to God's freeing work. Lazarus walked out of the tomb alive, but even in that moment of celebration, he was still shrouded in grave clothes. Jesus's instructions to "unbind him and let him go" reflect the need for us to maintain engagement in order to receive the whole gift of new life, no matter where we are in the emotional ups and downs of the process.

God weeps with us in the midst of darkness, staying with us on the emotional journey, and he persists in seeing us through to the resurrection. Staying with Jesus, authentic to our emotions along the way, brings the healing and transformation for which we long.

Physical Sensations

Relating thoughts and feelings to Christian flourishing may be familiar to us, but in Christian tradition, there is often less exploration of the physical body as related to our spiritual walk. This is one area where mindfulness has much to offer on the path of Christian discipleship. Mindfulness is a deeply physical experience, with a frequent emphasis on sensory awareness. Insomuch as our senses receive what is available from God in each moment, our senses can serve as pathways to God. Engagement with the senses is a way to experience the world that God has made.

Experiencing sensory input is different from *thinking about* sensory input. It takes only a split second for the body to move from a direct experience (such as warmth) to a cognitive interpretation of that experience (such as "that feels good"). Most of this cognitive interpretation is outside of our consciousness, and much of it is harmless. However, this quick shift from direct experience to cognition can pull us out of the present moment into thinking about the present moment.

With mindfulness, we practice staying with the *direct* experience of the moment. We tune in to the senses directly in order to experience what God has for us, without interference from our thoughts, judgments, and interpretations.

In light of the body's important role in mindfulness practice, let's take some time to break down the different types of sensory input one might experience during mindful awareness. Along the way, we will also explore how different senses might connect us with God.

TOUCH

Touch is thought to be the first sense to develop in utero,[8] and the ability to sense stimuli through the skin remains highly valuable as a conduit of information throughout life. Persons practicing mindfulness often become aware of touch sensations such as contact, pressure, temperature, or texture. For example, mindful awareness might include the feeling of toes in shoes or the sensation of air at the top of the scalp. Both formal and informal mindfulness practices include tuning in to these types of touch sensations we otherwise are prone to ignore in the course of daily life.

Touch is named explicitly in Scripture as a spiritual conduit. The Old Testament provides the Jewish people with detailed instructions regarding the altar, including "Whatever touches the altar shall become holy" (Exod 29:37). Endless instructions regarding what *not* to touch also are provided. Corpses, menstruating women, people with skin diseases, and various other "unclean" things are all proclaimed to be off-limits in the Old Testament context.

In the ministry of Jesus, touch is a conduit of healing. When a woman suffering from hemorrhaging heard about Jesus, she said to herself, "If I but touch his clothes, I will be made well" (Mark 5:28). And through touch, she was healed. When Jesus healed people of their blindness, muteness, and deafness, he often touched them in order to impart his healing power. As the Gospel of Mark puts it, "And wherever he went, into villages or cities or farms, they laid the sick in the marketplaces, and begged him that they might touch even the fringe of his cloak; and all who touched it were healed" (Mark 6:56).

So how does touch help us experience God today? The sense of touch is powerful in eliciting (or communicating) wonder, care, comfort, surprise, and many other emotions. We have to tune out most of these; otherwise, we would be overwhelmed by too much stimulation happening all at once. If you experience a sensory disorder with heightened sensitivity to touch, you know what I'm talking about!

But pausing to listen to some of that communication intentionally, in isolated doses, can allow for God's goodness to break through in powerful ways. We discover awe and wonder in the texture of tree bark, in the smoothness of an apple peel. There is stability and groundedness in the touch of clothing on the skin, in the physical contact with a chair holding you up. Through our attention to physical touch, God speaks to us and opens our hearts to worship.

SMELL

Every day, the olfactory system experiences a variety of smells, many of which have the potential to evoke strong emotional responses in us. The smell of freshly baked cookies can induce comfort. The smell of lavender can induce relaxation. The smell of a food we dislike can induce disgust or even anger.

Centuries before Christ, strong-smelling incense was used to symbolize prayers rising up to God—an offering commanded by God. Many branches of the church universal have continued this practice up to the present day. In these traditions, the smell of incense is an integral part of worship, a sensory pathway to awareness of God's presence.

For any of us, the experience of smell can cultivate emotion or inspire worship, especially when we are paying mindful attention. The multitude of smells with which God has infused our world are there to communicate something meaningful. In mindfulness practice, we tune in to the smells of life, discovering possibilities for deep gladness in the smell of a rainstorm or freshly washed clothes or a cup of chai or an old book. These beautiful smells are part of God's provision for us, made available in greater measure through the practice of mindful awareness.

HEARING

Once, Jesus's disciples asked him why he spoke in parables. "Seeing they do not perceive, and hearing they do not listen," Jesus replied, "nor do they understand" (Matt 13:13). It turns out that this hearing thing is really hard for us. We have a tendency to hear but not really hear, as well as to see but not really see.

We all know the difference between sound entering our ears and true hearing. I've been guilty of hearing the sound of my husband talking without actually hearing his words. This is a failure of active listening, and this is how we tend to operate— lost in our own thoughts and challenged to be fully engaged outside our orb of self-consciousness. It is entirely possible and all too easy to go through life hearing sounds but not taking time to absorb them. For those walking with Jesus, they heard and saw him at work but had difficulty hearing and absorbing his words.

In mindfulness practice, we can literally tune our sense of hearing; we can absorb, we can *listen*. When we listen well, we are responding to Jesus's familiar exhortation "Let anyone with ears to hear listen!" (Mark 4:9). Listening well, using our ears to hear, means we are opening another passageway for God to commune with us. And opening our ears, we lay aside preconceived notions about what we might hear, ready to receive through our sense of hearing what God has for us. Hearing literal sounds, then, serves as one pathway for hearing and understanding God with the heart.

TASTE

What do you love to taste? The psalmist writes, "O taste and see that the Lord is good" (Ps 34:8). Take a moment to identify one taste you enjoy—something you really look forward to tasting. This is God's goodness. Can we really taste the Lord's goodness? Literally? As a mindfulness practitioner, I would say yes, literally. Good tastes are tastes of God's goodness. God has, in fact, filled up our world with the goodness of delicious tastes and a host of other unnecessarily pleasant experiences. Why does food taste so amazing? Why are flowers colorful and multi-shaped? Why are there happy feelings, even when we do nothing to deserve them? Why is there such glorious, beautiful diversity in the human race?

These questions have no answer. It appears that God has woven goodness and beauty into the design of his world as a pure gift to us. Sure, some of these pleasant experiences also serve a functional role in species survival, but God certainly could have chosen a less pleasurable system.

My department recently hosted an open house in which free food and therapy dogs filled the classroom hallways. Students on break from class came upon the event with surprise and joy on their faces. "Why is this happening?" exclaimed one student. "Because life is amazing!" replied another exuberantly, as she filled her plate with delicious-tasting food. Amen, sister. Life is amazing!

As with all mindfulness practice, our awareness of taste does not aim to find only the pleasant. We open up our awareness and pay attention to whatever is there. Taste is a lovely example of learning to receive goodness through the pleasant and unpleasant. I find the taste of raw broccoli to be quite unpleasant, yet I know it is good for me, so I eat it anyway. Sometimes when we taste the Lord's goodness, it is bitter, and we don't look forward to another bite. Yet the goodness is there in so many tastes, whether we like them or not. God is at work in all of the moments of life. We can use mindfulness to lean into each moment and be curious about how goodness might show up for us in the sense of taste.

SIGHT

The psalms are filled with sensory awareness, including awareness of visual input: "See that the Lord is good," said the psalmist (Ps 34:8), reminding us that sight is another way that God imparts his goodness to us. Sight is how God absorbed the goodness of creation at the very beginning. We find this beautiful refrain in the first chapter of Genesis: "And God saw that it was good," repeated several times and ending in verse 31 with "God saw everything that he had made, and indeed, it was very good." God *saw* the goodness.

As with other senses, we are often tempted to *think* about what we see—to label and interpret and analyze, instead of staying with a direct visual experience. But mindful awareness is the practice of experiencing shapes and colors without the filter of thought. We take in visual stimuli and experience them as directly as possible, apart from language. We set aside judgments and enter into the pure experience available through the eyes.

When using mindfulness practice to open ourselves to God's goodness through the sense of sight, it is not with the goal of having any particular response. We do not need to have pleasurable feelings or profound thoughts when we pay attention to sight. The goal is simply to be present to God's creation through the experience of seeing, trusting that God's goodness will be present there, no matter what we feel or think. God doesn't rely on us to judge the creation as good in order for it to be good. It is simply true that God is good, and that when we use our sense of sight to explore God's good creation, we are attending to something that matters to God. This is an act of worship—to tune in to our sense of sight and explore the colors and shapes of God's creation.

Cognitive and verbal attributions of goodness often fall flat. My artist friend does not feel encouraged if I see a painting of hers and only say, "Good job," moving on quickly to the next conversation item. To provide authentic encouragement, I have to dwell with her work and truly see it—to notice which color blue she chose and how the symmetry of the piece makes me feel, to acknowledge the time that she put into the creation. Appreciation is expressed when I take the time to see and experience her artwork.

So it is with God. When we take time to truly see God's creation without snap judgments, we are offering praise. We are offering God the gift of our full, visual attention to God's marvelous work. And in the process, we are opening ourselves up to receiving the goodness with which God has infused our visual world.

ACKNOWLEDGING OUR LIMITS

We've looked together at the five senses and the role of sensory awareness in mindful Christianity, but what happens if you do not have access to one or more of the senses, either in part or in full? Perhaps you experience a visual or hearing impairment. Perhaps your sense of smell and/or taste is limited, or nerve damage prevents a full experience of touch in some way. Perhaps you experience neurological issues that alter and distort your sensory experience.

With mindfulness, we practice *radical acceptance* of these limitations. We acknowledge that all of us have limits in some form at some time, and we practice working with our limits skillfully. I do not say this lightly. Mindfulness never minimizes the true pain of our limits. Limits are often frightening and frustrating, and it is a natural response to fight against our limits. As a friend said about a young girl's incurable deafness, "How could one ever accept a thing like that?"

Here is where our belief in God's goodness is illuminated. To practice mindfulness within a Christian framework, we do not need to like our limits or approve of them. We do not need to appreciate them, grow through them, or find a silver lining. We do not need to use positive thinking or expect a miracle cure or even feel hopeful. Any of these things may or may not result when we practice mindfulness in God's presence. The goal, though, is to notice resistance, practice awareness of whatever sensory input is there to be found, and acknowledge that God is here. God will take care of the rest, in God's own time and way.

Thus, mindful awareness allows us to honor our limits along the way while staying present to each moment, tuned in to God's world and trusting that it is truly "good," just as he declared it to be at creation's birth.

Behaviors and Urges

Urges are another salient experience of the present moment, along with behaviors in response to those urges. Our relationship with urges is key to the development of self-control and healthy habits. We sometimes battle and argue with urges, either overcoming or giving in with our behavior. We sometimes welcome urges and follow joyfully. Sometimes we choose to ignore them, and they go away.

Some behavioral responses to urges cause harm in almost any context, such as using drugs or punching someone in the face. Some are likely to cause benefit in almost any context, such as taking a deep breath or considering another person's perspective. But many urges and behaviors have no obvious harm or benefit; they are simply the movements of our mind and body that carry us through each day.

For those of us struggling with addiction, the relationship with urges has become overpowering. Urges have felt out of control, inseparable from behaviors, with destructive effects on health, relationships, employment, or happiness. When our urges lead to uncontrolled behaviors in areas of substances, sex, or violence, we can find ourselves (and those around us) in deep suffering.

Learning to observe our urges and our automatic responses to those urges is a component of mindfulness practice. We notice the urges rising and passing, like waves; this is sometimes called "urge surfing." We learn to work with urges skillfully, giving ourselves other options besides mindless behavioral submission.

During a mindfulness meditation exercise, many urges will arise. Most of them are small, such as the urge to move position, scratch an itch, or stop a meditation. These urges are not necessarily problematic; they are not good or bad. When we practice mindfulness, we notice our different options in responding to these urges. We pause to notice the urges, and we give ourselves time to observe our autopilot attempting to kick in. We practice watching the urge fluctuate, and we practice intentional responses to the urge.

If my knee is itching, for example, my unconscious impulse is to move my hand and scratch it. But during mindfulness practice, I first notice the urge. I might let my awareness rest on the physical sensation for a bit and notice the pull on my hand to move toward my knee. I observe the shape, size, and quality of the sensation in my knee. I recognize the thoughts and feelings associated with the sensation—perhaps a belief that I cannot resist the urge to scratch my knee, along with a feeling of mild anxiety. In some cases, I might choose to go ahead and scratch my knee, maintaining awareness of the sensation of my hand moving and the result this achieves. Does it relieve the discomfort? Or simply change it or prolong it?

This type of observation of urges and behaviors in the moment frees us up to be intentional, more in control of our actions. It gives us information about the effectiveness of our responses to urges. This is a helpful skill to cultivate if we want to be effective in managing ourselves, both physically and emotionally. It allows us to assess our responses accurately to see if they are effectively accomplishing our goals.

We are encouraged in Scripture to cultivate self-control, a fruit of the Spirit (Gal 5:23). When we use mindfulness to observe and temper urges and behaviors, we are doing just that: cultivating self-control. Mindfulness is a tool to help us set aside our automatic, human responses in order to open space for new responses. From a Christian perspective, this provides time for us to hear God's leading and opens us up to follow God's leading, rather than mindlessly giving in to our impulses. Hitting pause helps us be intentional with our choices, which helps us be intentional in our Christian walk.

Observing urges and behaviors does not result in some perfect form of self-management. It simply increases our awareness of the way we are responding to ourselves and our environment so that we can know what we are doing when we are doing it. Through this increased intentionality, mindfulness opens up the possibility of kindness and compassion toward ourselves and others in each moment. It helps us to see and follow God's leading as we walk through life fully aware.

Throughout this chapter, we have explored several aspects of present-moment awareness—thoughts, feelings, physical sensations, and urges/behaviors. All of these experiences are part of God's created order, and we can access them in each moment to be more in tune with all that God is doing. When we take time to pause in God's presence and to notice these small aspects of present-moment experience, we access the calming and restorative power of mindfulness.

Living the Practice: What's in the Moment?

Set aside approximately five minutes to be curious about your present-moment experiences. Set a timer. On a blank piece of paper, create four columns (or sections) labeled as follows: thoughts, feelings, physical sensations, and behaviors/urges. Until the timer goes off, write down everything you observe in these four categories, moment to moment. Approach this exercise in the way a scientist gathers a fascinating data set.

If you're having trouble distinguishing between thoughts and feelings, you might notice that emotions tend to be one word (like *anxious* or *peaceful*), while thoughts tend to come in strings of words (like "I can't take this" or "Things seem to be going well right now"). Be aware of any urge to analyze or interpret what you notice, and come back to direct observation of your experience in the moment. Don't worry if you run out of things to write; you are just practicing observing whatever is there, staying curious along the way.

Once your timer has gone off, review your list to see if you have accurately categorized the different elements of your experience. For example, under feelings, if you wrote *unsure*, notice if this was an emotion or if it was actually a thought, like "I am unsure about what I'm supposed to be doing here." If it was an unsure feeling combined with a thought about that, allow this to be reflected in both sections.

In this way, you are practicing accurate observation of your present-moment experience. You can carry this skill into your formal mindfulness practices and also into your informal mindful awareness each day. ■

Life-changing gratitude does not fasten to a life unless nailed through with one very specific nail at a time.

—Ann Voskamp[1]

CHAPTER 6

UNCEASING, GRATEFUL PRAYER

I am in my Father, and you in me, and I in you.
John 14:20

Prayer and Awareness

Prayer has always been a bit of a challenge for me. I'm an introvert who does not love expounding on my needs and experiences with visible companions. Even more challenging is articulating my needs to an invisible God. I sit down to pray and know how to go through the motions (gratitude, intercession, confession, praise, etc.), but I run out of stuff to say and get bored quickly. Talking is not my preferred mode of connection. As a result, I don't pray formally very often.

Mindfulness has radically transformed my ability to pray. When combined with an awareness of God's presence, mindfulness is prayer—abiding in the present moment, where

God is, with intention to listen, observe, cultivate awe, and receive. Perhaps to "pray without ceasing" (1 Thess 5:17) means this ongoing awareness of the divine work throughout each day.

There are three approaches to cultivating mindful prayer (or prayerful mindfulness):

- **Informal, mindful awareness throughout each day in God's presence.** This is a prayerful posture as we make ourselves open and available to notice God's creation.

- **Formal meditation in God's presence.** The silence and open stance of formal mindfulness meditation open us up to deeper spiritual connection, softening our resistance to connecting with God as we lessen the power of distracting thoughts and observe the moment.

- **Integration of Centering Prayer principles into mindfulness practice.** This uses God's presence as the focus of attention, in the same way that we cultivate awareness of other present-moment experiences through traditional mindfulness practice.

These three paths of prayerful mindfulness serve to deepen and sustain our connection to God. Each path serves as a method of cultivating wonder at God's creation and increasing awareness of the many ways we are sustained by God in every moment we are alive.

Prayerful mindfulness is staying present with Jesus. The night before his death, in the Garden of Gethsemane, Jesus asked his disciples to "remain here, and stay awake with me" (Matt 26:36–46). He was fully and authentically present to his emotions on that night, "grieved and agitated," in deep turmoil. And in the midst of this intense, divine drama, he made one simple request of his disciples: stay awake. It turned out that the disciples were unable to follow this request, and they slept instead. They were not present to their emotions or to Jesus.

So now it's our turn to stay awake with Jesus. What does that look like? It looks like being conscious and present with God, tuned in to the divine drama that is playing out within and around us. It looks like prayerfulness; it looks like mindfulness. Could there possibly be anything more fulfilling, more satisfying, than staying awake with God? Mindfulness is this practice of being fully awake, so we don't sleep through life and miss out on what God is doing. In this sense, Christian mindfulness is a form of prayer.

Gratitude and Attention

Gratitude is another ceaseless act asked of us by Scripture. "Give thanks in all circumstances," the apostle Paul writes, "for this is the will of God in Christ Jesus for you" (1 Thess 5:18). It can be easier to focus attention on what we do not have, to "complain in all circumstances" rather than give thanks. Yet God's will for us is to give thanks.

A prerequisite for giving thanks is seeing the gifts that are before us. Mindfulness helps with this; it is a tool for noticing the gifts of life and then reaching out to receive what has been offered. Through mindful, nonjudgmental awareness of the present moment, our eyes are opened to see the beauty and goodness in each moment of life.

Even without Christian faith, mindfulness creates the conditions for gratitude. But Christian practitioners also acknowledge the gift-giver, placing the world's goodness and its pain within the context of a divine relationship. Paying attention to divine creation and provision, we get to know the maker and flourish in that caring and intimate relationship.

Gratitude is not an emotion to be manufactured, but a basic acknowledgment that each moment of life is enough, no matter what our experience, and that we are provided for. Some moments are pleasant, some unpleasant. Some are painful, some are filled with joy. Yet through all of our moments, we have what we need. When we resist our experience, believing that life is not okay as it is, we multiply the normal pain of life and create additional suffering. But when we accept our lives exactly as they are, without having to change anything, we form a natural bridge to feelings of gratitude.

One of the best thank-yous I've ever received for a gift was from my one-year-old nephew, a person too small to talk. How did he say thank you without words? He looked at the gift for a very long time. He examined every nook and cranny of the elephant pull toy, swiveling the ears and pointing his tiny pointer finger at each color. He turned the wheels with curiosity. He gazed up in his mom's face, smiling and pointing her attention to the new toy. He gestured for her to unwrap it and then took more time to point, examine, and smile. His gratitude overflowed, and my heart as a giver was warmed.

This tiny, wordless human was practicing mindfulness. He centered his full, direct attention on one thing in the moment. He was unencumbered by the filter of language, experiencing the object in a pure form rather than getting lost in interpretations, analysis, or judgments.

All of life is a gift—every thing in every moment, the pleasant and unpleasant. Nothing is off-limits for our attention. In every moment, we have the opportunity to really gaze at the gift, as this one-year-old did, to experience the gift without expectation, interpretation, analysis, or judgment. When we do this, the heart settles and peace grows. Imagine the warmth this brings to God's giver heart, as we enter into a full experience of what God has lavished on us in the moment.

Here are some recent examples of mindful awareness in my life that flowed naturally into prayerful gratitude:

- I cut a red onion in half. I saw the vibrant colors inside, alternating reds and whites, and the moisture dripping out. I acknowledged that this gorgeous piece of edible goodness had been grown with patience and then transported all the way to my kitchen counter by a host of dedicated individuals.

- I opened the blinds on a dark winter morning and could not see outside because the window was covered with ice. Gazing intently, I saw intricate and beautiful patterns, feathered swirls that shimmered and caught the light of the street lamp outside. This was art, delivered freely to my bedroom window as I slept through the night.

- I was flooded with angry emotions and paused to notice my irrational thoughts and painful feelings. I turned with mindful intention to look in the face of the other person. I saw their physical features and their humanity, and I noticed that we were together. I noticed how their face told a story different from my expectation, and my self-critical narrative changed in an instant. My heart softened, and I smiled.

The examples are endless, because the moments of our life are too many to count. The sheer extravagance of God, in giving us so many moments, so many gifts, is staggering. The gifts are there, if we but take time to receive. In this way, mindfulness has the capacity to be an act of ceaseless, grateful prayer.

Curiosity

The stage for gratitude is set by curiosity, a key component of mindful awareness. Curiosity is an "inquisitive, wondering, ready to poke around and figure something out" attitude.[2] It incorporates eagerness to learn and grow.

Being curious about the world can come quite naturally when we encounter something new or novel. Experiences that defy our expectation often elicit surprise and pique curiosity. But it's easy to stop being curious about the world when experiences don't feel new anymore, and we easily forget that every moment is actually brand new and unpredictable.

Thinking we know what to expect puts us in autopilot, and this has the benefit of helping us get through the logistics of life more efficiently. Staying uncurious embodies an attitude of "I know this already, so I can act quickly." However, it can also dull the senses, reduce accuracy, and restrict learning. For this reason, cultivating curiosity in the midst of everyday life has immense benefit for our sense of well-being and our effectiveness in the world.

Young children are often very curious about the small details of their world, which is why the most fascinating playthings can be the most ordinary. A box, pan, cardboard tube, or mud puddle can hold deep fascination for the young. And what emerges is not just learning; it is also joy and playfulness. Toddlers think the most ordinary things are absolutely hilarious. Like comedians, they can help us pause to notice the things we take for granted, learning about our own habits as we find humor in the process.

As children grow into elementary school age and beyond, they sometimes go through a period of thinking they know everything. No matter what they are shown or asked to do, the response is "I know." While this can be a natural phase of independence and confidence building, it can make learning more difficult. The closed, dismissive, uninterested attitude creates barriers to learning, to joyful engagement with life, and to connecting with other people. Curiosity is harder when we think nothing is new anymore.

Mindful curiosity is a return to the wide-eyed awareness of young childhood. We don't have to make up this newness, because every moment really *is* new. Take, for example, the sight of a tree. Every tree is unique, shifting and changing in each moment due to weather, wildlife, growth, decay, and other factors. So if I want to actually see a tree as it is, not as I think I know it to be, I will slow down and get curious in the moment with the tree. Curiosity about the tree in front of me gives me better information about present-moment reality than the tree image in my mind. It also stimulates joy. In our curious exploration of the world, we encounter surprises that get us smiley, awe filled, and prayerfully grateful to our creator God.

Mindful awareness stimulates a revolving cycle of gratitude and curiosity that, for the Christian, stimulates prayer throughout each day. Through never-ending curiosity, Christian mindfulness wakes us up to the wonder of God's creation, and our response to that so often leads to grateful prayer. Mindfulness helps us to pray.

Living the Practice: Nurturing Gratitude and Body Acceptance

You are invited now to explore the practice of curious, mindful attentiveness as a way of cultivating appreciation for your own body—an act that can be approached as prayerful gratitude, if you choose.

For this practice, choose one body part, such as your feet, fingers, or nose. Start with a body part about which your feelings are neutral or positive, rather than one that tends to elicit self-criticism. Take some time to fully explore this part of your body as if you are encountering it for the very first time. Engage your full powers of observational curiosity to learn everything you can about it. Without judgment, explanation, or interpretation, take some time to pay attention to the following:

- Shape

- Color

- Symmetries and asymmetries

- Various components (for example, muscle, bone, skin)

- Function (what it does for you)

- Movement (both voluntary and involuntary)

You may notice a tendency for your mind to generate thoughts about this particular body part—whether you like it or not, what other people might think of it, how well it works for you, or what you might do to improve it. When you notice you have been swept away in thoughts, gently return to direct and curious observation of what you can experience with your senses.

Notice that you are engaging in this mindful awareness in the presence of God, who created your body and pronounced it good.

See if it is possible to appreciate this part of your body and what it has done for you, noticing your body as part of God's amazing and wonderful creation. ■

Most of us spend so much time thinking about where we have been or where we are supposed to be going that we have a hard time recognizing where we actually are. When someone asks us where we want to be in our lives, the last thing that occurs to us is to look down at our feet and say, "Here, I guess, since this is where I am."

—*Barbara Brown Taylor*[1]

CHAPTER 7

LEARNING CONTENTMENT

So we do not lose heart. Even though our outer nature is wasting away,
our inner nature is being renewed day by day.
2 Corinthians 4:16

Releasing Resistance, Finding Contentment

Since the fall of humanity in the garden of Eden, people have been tempted by the belief that they do not have enough and that they are not enough. We have trouble grasping the possibility of being content with what we have and who we are, often believing we could be much happier if our circumstances were different. We are lured, each in our own way, toward false promises of happiness through false idols of appearance, status, and money.

Both Scripture and scientific research confirm that, in fact, a very small percentage of our happiness has to do with circumstance. How else could such an amazing statement as the apostle Paul's be made? He said, "Therefore I am content with weaknesses, insults, hardships, persecutions, and calamities for the sake of Christ; for whenever I am weak, then I am strong" (2 Cor 12:10).

According to a meta-analysis of studies on happiness,[2] circumstances account for only 10 percent of the variability in happiness levels between people. In other words, circumstances and happiness level are not highly correlated with one another. Of much greater significance are heritability (accounting for 50 percent) and intentional activity (40 percent). This means that a good portion of our happiness, our contentment, our sense of well-being has to do with our response to our circumstances.

Mindfulness is one of those "intentional activities" that research points to as having the potential to open us up to contentment. Through mindfulness, we stop insisting that God give us a different life than the one we have, and we choose to accept our reality for what it is. This is "radical acceptance": letting go of the need to change anything, even in the most difficult of circumstances, as a pathway to contentment. We open our eyes to see God in the very circumstances where we find ourselves, and we open our hands to receive all that God has for us.

Acceptance is not a term to be thrown around lightly. There are many painful circumstances in life: violence, relationship loss, terminal illness, racism, discrimination, depression, and numerous others. It is clear that things are not right and that our world is filled with pain. Scripture reminds us, "We know that the whole creation has been groaning in labor pains until now; and not only the creation, but we ourselves, who have the first fruits of the Spirit, groan inwardly while we wait for adoption, the redemption of our bodies." (Rom 8:22–23). The experience of pain is universal.

I see these inevitable life pains as an elderly friend of mine experiences the death of several dear friends and family members in his aging cohort. He is watching the progression of dementia in many who live around him in his retirement community, seeing and sharing their anxiety about losing memory and perception. There is inherent fear in these losses of aging, and he is boldly voicing questions such as "What will happen to me if I no longer know who I am?" So when he asks me what mindfulness has to offer someone his age, I do not take this question lightly. How can we accept these impairments of aging, these deep losses, in ourselves and in those we love? How do we live with the realities of past, current, and future pain?

That last concern is perhaps most poignant: How do we live, knowing that pain is coming? As the author of Ecclesiastes cheerfully reminds us:

> Again I saw that under the sun the race is not to the swift, nor the battle to the strong, nor bread to the wise, nor riches to the intelligent, nor favor to the skillful; but time and chance happen to them all. For no one can anticipate the time of disaster. Like fish taken in a cruel net, and like birds caught in a snare, so mortals are snared at a time of calamity, when it suddenly falls upon them. (Eccl 9:11–12)

This Scripture passage, like most other Bible verses about suffering, does not appear on lists of encouraging verses to read during times of pain. (Typically, we do not try to cheer one another up by saying, "Calamity is on the way, no matter what you do!") But our life experiences support this; nothing stays pleasant forever. In this life, we experience ups and downs, and no one can avoid a constant fluctuation of fortune and emotion.

So how is it that Paul can describe himself as content? He writes, "I have learned to be content with whatever I have. I know what it is to have little, and I know what it is to have plenty. In any and all circumstances I have learned the secret of being well-fed and of going hungry, of having plenty and of being in need. I can do all things through him who strengthens me" (Phil 4:11–13). Truth be told, most of us have complained about far less difficult circumstances than Paul experienced. Even the small sufferings of our days can be hard to bear; challenges like internet outages, rainy weather, and annoying people can be quite a blow to our sense of well-being. Humans are master complainers, and for most of us, nothing is ever quite right. Yet Paul points out that contentment is a very real possibility, even in circumstances such as having little, being hungry, and being in need. In doing so, he paves the way for a Christian understanding of mindful acceptance—learning to be content in every circumstance.

Good Christian theology grounds us in the reality of God's provision amid life's sufferings. We can know without a doubt that God is faithful through our hard times, no matter what happens. God gives us what we need in each moment and refines our character in the fire of suffering. God blesses us with unexpected goodness along the way and assures us of the hope of heaven when the trials of this earth are over.

We can know this, but our most natural response in a moment of unpleasantness is to ignore it or push it away. Our resistance often flows out of fear of inadequacy or future suffering. I might resist feeling grief because I fear being overwhelmed, resist thinking about past mistakes because I fear feelings of guilt, or resist looking in the mirror because I fear feelings of shame.

Consciously or unconsciously, I push away my experience in the moment as an attempt to avoid suffering.

At the same time, we are prone to resist even the pleasant moments. Pleasant experiences can bring joy, which can bring fear of losing that joy. In this way, joy can be the most vulnerable feeling of all, sparking resistance in the same way as unpleasant emotions.[3] Or sometimes we are just unaware of how good the moment is. I chuckle every time I remember my cousin demanding that his four-year-old daughter eat a piece of cake that he knew she would love, while she resisted with all her might.

Resistance can take many forms. Sometimes it is avoidance of a thought, person, place, or emotion. Sometimes it shows up as a denial of reality. Sometimes it is spacing out, being tired, or oversleeping. Sometimes resistance is overthinking, analyzing, interpreting, or judging. Sometimes it is busyness. In this modern age, resistance often manifests as technology use—numbing out our discomfort by looking at screens.

Resistance blocks us from accessing all of the information about a moment. Have you ever been surprised by an emotion you didn't know was there? Maybe you found tension in your shoulders and realized you were stressed, or when someone said a kind word, you found unexpected tears in your eyes. It can be a challenge to remain connected to our experiences, and this makes it difficult to care well for ourselves.

Some types of resistance have their place, and resistance can be a natural reaction to the unpleasantness of life. If I am attacked in a dark alley, I hope for a fight-or-flight response that helps me resist the attack and escape safely. The goal of mindfulness is not to turn off all resistance, but to become more aware of how well resistance is (or is not) working for us.

Within a Christian framework, releasing resistance to the present moment is an acknowledgment that we are not God. To welcome the present moment exactly as it is equates to giving up our insistence about how life should be and becoming aware of God's divine provision. We are not responsible for any of this provision to happen; we are not the creators of our own blessing, and there is nothing we can do to change God's faithfulness. All we can do is choose whether or not we drop our resistance and turn in the moment toward the God who loves us in order to receive God's gifts of goodness. This is where mindfulness and Christian theology flow together in beautiful harmony to cultivate contentment.

Resisting present-moment experience is one of the ways the mind creates its own suffering. An ancient formula in the mindfulness tradition is this:

$$\text{Pain} \times \text{Resistance} = \text{Suffering}$$

How does this multiplication happen? In the process of resisting pain, we try to understand and analyze it. This keeps us connected to negative thoughts as we pull up past examples and project future examples of pain, perhaps blaming ourselves (or others) for everything that could have been done differently. And because this negative looping of the mind happens largely unaware, we remain stuck until the cycle can be interrupted.

Mindfulness practice interrupts the suffering-inducing cycle of resistance. It allows us to observe the architecture of the mind with curiosity, noticing the fascinating and even humorous tendency we have to resist reality by overthinking. It's truly amazing how quickly we can move down a resistant and judgmental thought chain: "I don't understand this lecture. . . . I'm going to fail the test. . . . My life is worthless." Mindfulness allows us to increase awareness of these types of rapid-acting thought chains and to develop skill in creating new mental structures: "I don't understand this lecture. . . . It's okay to struggle. . . . I'm going to ask for help." Over time, as we practice, we are less likely to fall into self-destructive mental traps. And when we do succumb, mindfulness helps us to walk away more effectively.

We can think of resistance as an unproductive power struggle with reality. This strain, this wasted effort, is ubiquitous in our human experience. We tense ourselves in resistance to all types of mild (and major) discomforts, real or imagined. In doing so, we add to our suffering unnecessarily. When I lay awake on a sleepless night, I find my forehead creased with tension. When my child acts up in public, I find my mind fixated on what his next behavior will be. When my spouse appears tired, I find my defenses on high alert because he might be mad at me. When I walk through a snowstorm, I find my body and mind tensed in response to the cold. These are all real-life challenges that only become more challenging through my resistance. In some ways, these are challenges largely *because* of my resistance.

There are certain times that the effort of striving is very productive. I can sometimes find God's goodness when I push myself a little harder on the yoga mat or sit with awkwardness in an important conversation or stay a little later at work to finish up that difficult project. But more often than not, the striving is not helpful. Sometimes I need to let myself come out of that yoga pose early or take a time-out in an escalating conversation or wrap up a project at the "good enough" stage rather than the "perfect" stage.

How do I know the difference between generative effort and mindless striving? There's no fail-proof rule for that. But the only wisdom available comes from the power of noticing—noticing my striving and taking stock of the results. Is this hard work that I'm doing a way of living into God's good gifts? Or am I acting out of fear or self-loathing or self-importance? Am I receiving what God has for me in this moment? Or am I avoiding a full experience of life by avoiding some aspect of the present moment?

It turns out that abundant life is not achieved through striving—through avoiding, resisting, or even changing what is present. It is achieved through opening ourselves up to God's existing abundance in the moment. In the process, we find that many of the unwanted and unpleasant things change on their own. And the challenges that stick around become less important in light of God's ever-present provision. In this way, mindfulness is the practice of contentment.

What does this look like in real life? A client of mine was struggling through issues of personal identity and values, and she was encountering significant friction with her family along the way. Her political and religious convictions seemed at deep odds with those of her parents, and she felt negative judgment from them about her evolving viewpoints. Direct conversations about big questions like sexual orientation and biblical interpretation were taboo in her family culture, and this silence was feeding into her symptoms of depression and anxiety. She loved her family but also felt deeply wounded by her interactions with them. She dreaded going home because of feeling unseen, misunderstood, judged, and uncared for in the midst of her own struggle to understand and care for herself during times of pain.

At the root of the healing journey for this individual was the cultivation of mindful acceptance. She did not need to like her family culture or agree with her parents' assessment of her failings. She did not need to look forward to going home, and she did not need to pretend she wasn't hurt. Mindful acceptance meant that she could acknowledge the reality of her family relationships as they were. Fighting against the way things were—beating her head against the wall of reality—did not change the reality. Through the practice of mindfulness, she learned to accept that "what is here is already here" and to lay down the resistance to her reality that was exacerbating depression and anxiety. This cultivation of acceptance freed her up to take better care of her wounded emotions and to feel less distressed when she interacted with family.

For us also, mindful acceptance provides an option of practicing contentment in all circumstances by welcoming each moment as enough. With mindfulness, we do not suspend our welcome until a moment proves itself worthy. We extend our welcome to each present-moment experience, whether pleasant or unpleasant, with openness and curiosity. In doing so, we welcome God and say yes to God's ever-flowing provision in our lives.

Provision

A beautiful picture of God's provision is painted for us in John's Gospel, with the account of Jesus feeding a crowd in the wilderness (John 6:1–14). Five thousand people followed Jesus into the wilderness to hear him teach. When they got hungry, it was obvious that there was not enough money or food available to feed them. His disciple Philip responded to the need with reality-based hopelessness: "Six months' wages would not buy enough bread for each of them to get a little." But disciple Andrew had a different point of view. He saw what *was* available in the moment—five loaves and two fish brought by a boy—and he brought that small amount to Jesus. Jesus, ever the one to think outside of the box of possibilities, used that little bit of food to feed the huge crowd of people. It turned out that there was enough, with twelve baskets of bread left over.

Bound by their expectations of what "enough" would look like, neither Philip nor Andrew had a mental framework for anticipating this miracle. But Andrew was able to *see* the little bit of food that was there in the moment and present that to Jesus. Miracles often happen this way. Rather than swooping in to turn our circumstances upside down out of the blue, God waits for us to notice what is there and to bring it to him. For a miracle to happen, we have to first see the raw materials in the moment.

This is where mindfulness comes in. Through radical acceptance, we know that what we have is enough in the hands of God, even when we don't know *how* it is enough. We often can't see the solution ourselves. But we open our eyes to what is available in the moment and then present it to God.

In my own experiences of silent meditation, I sometimes can be surprised to discover a rushing flood of thoughts raging against my circumstances. Perceived injustices, challenges, and to-dos dominate my awareness in a torrential downpour of discontented thoughts. In light of this thought onslaught, paying attention to the present moment feels almost impossible. As my body quietly engages the moment, it is shocking how loud my mind remains. Then, in those meditative moments, this "not enough" thought stream is what I bring to Jesus, along with whatever else mindful awareness surfaces in that moment. I can bring these meager provisions from my moment to God in expectancy that God will use them to provide abundantly more than I could ever ask or imagine (Eph 3:20).

So mindfulness practices, both formal and informal, open us up to the miracle, providing "raw material" for God's miraculous work. If I resist my experience in the moment because I am afraid of scarcity or pain or danger, I close myself off from the miracle. If I notice whatever is in the moment, I bring it to God, and God does an unexpected transformative miracle. And it always turns out to be enough.

Seeing the Resurrection

Amazingly, God is performing miracles in each moment, whether or not we can see them. The resurrection story is a poignant reminder of how often we are oblivious to God's miracles. The disciples had seen Lazarus being raised from the dead (we talked about this in chapter 5), as well as a host of other miracles, and they had heard Jesus predict his own return from the dead. But by the time Jesus was crucified, the disciples had already forgotten about resurrection possibility. They were unaware of anything at work as his body lay in the tomb. At the very time that Jesus was resurrected, his disciples were hiding fearfully in a locked room, terrified and hopeless.

But even in that darkest of spaces, beyond their ability to see or believe, Jesus was at that moment rising from the dead. Resurrection was happening, in the dark, without any action or even faith required from the disciples.

This sets the stage for mindful awareness. The darkness is not dangerous, nor are our feelings of terror and hopelessness. These are passing experiences that emerge sometimes while God's resurrection is at work. God does not always take away our suffering—our unpleasant emotions, our despair, or our fear. Instead, God enters into them and does resurrection work right there in the darkness, sometimes even in secret.

So we can lean into each present-moment experience, pleasant or unpleasant, with the knowledge that no matter how bleak things appear, morning will come again because God is at work. We will always have all that we need. In words attributed to Frederick Buechner, "Resurrection means that the worst thing is never the last thing."[4]

From a Christian perspective, mindfulness supports us in finding God *within* our terror and despair, rather than looking outside of them. We see this in the example of Mary Magdalene, the follower of Jesus who walked *to* Jesus's tomb at the earliest opportunity after his burial, even before knowing about the resurrection. She was open and ready for the miracle of resurrection, while Jesus's disciples hid away in fear. In this same way, mindfulness is a method by which we can "practice resurrection,"[5] being fully aware and fully alive in each of the moments we have been given, even when we're not yet sure how the provision we need will emerge. Christian mindfulness practice is a full embrace of the resurrection life—an opportunity to welcome each moment God gives us, even during times of darkness, and to bring all that we find in each moment to God in full faith that it is enough.

Everything Changes

There is one area of life in which it is particularly easy to become resistant and miss God's good work: change. Change is challenging for humans. We long for stability. Uncertainty of any type puts strain on us. Even positive change creates stress, because so many unknowns are involved. Getting married, having a child, buying a house, getting a promotion—these types of changes can be exciting but also quite difficult.

This is unfortunate, because change is a constant. Every single moment of life is different from every other moment; no two moments are the same. Our bodies are in constant change, as are our thoughts, feelings, circumstances, and environments. There are similarities between moments, for sure, and repetitions of themes. But we never breathe the same breath twice or see the same sunrise more than once.

Change is actually good for happiness, because it keep things fresh and new, just the way we need them so we feel curious and alive. Something that is life-giving can lose its luster if we never change it up.[6] The constant change inherent in life delivers the surprise needed for joy and the challenge needed for growth. It stretches us out of our comfort zone, so we can learn new things and gain mastery.

So how do we live with mixed feelings about change? Change is necessary and beneficial, yet it sparks resistance. Our option—our invitation—is to lean into change and make friends with it. We don't just tolerate it; we open ourselves to it and get curious, becoming aware of resistance and letting it go. We intentionally ride the waves of change along with God.

Embracing change does not mean we are haplessly flailing in the wind. Think of it more as learning to hold on for the ride, leaning into the adventure with courage and tenacity. When I was younger, I found airplane takeoffs quite terrifying. They were loud and bumpy, and they felt out of control. I would use deep breathing to calm myself, and no harm was done. But as I got older, I tried a new technique: tuning in to the power of flying. I was not in the pilot's seat (thank goodness for all on board!), but I grounded my attention in the wonder of flight. The plane, with its wings outstretched, was lifting off the ground and soaring into the air with power and purpose. Sure, there were bumps and wobbles along the way, but tuning in to the power of takeoff was exhilarating. I was flying!

This shift in my attitude toward flight transformed airplane takeoffs from something tolerable to something exciting. I learned to look forward to those moments of becoming airborne and soaring into the sky, even if some terror remained. Wow, flying! What a wonder to be a part of such a strong and amazing moment.

When we embrace change, we are making this same shift. The change is no longer something to tolerate or resist. Instead, it becomes something to which we harness our energy. Even though we cannot control much of our change, and even though we might feel terror, we can lean into the adventure and experience the full exhilaration of the ride.

Through mindfulness, we are also practicing a connection with something more constant than the fluctuations of each moment. A common metaphor for this is the ocean. The ocean is a vast and deep body of water, difficult for our minds to comprehend. You can imagine the surface of the ocean being in constant fluctuation. Sometimes stormy weather creates big waves on the surface, a churning that can bring down big ships or a tsunami that can overpower whole villages. Sometimes calm weather creates smooth sailing conditions, and sunshine glitters on the surface of the water. But no matter the weather on top, the ocean is much bigger than the surface. It is deep and diverse and powerful. Its identity is unmoved by changing weather patterns. The surface of the ocean may change, but the ocean is much deeper than the surface.

The surface of the ocean is like our thoughts, feelings, physical sensations, and circumstances. We experience constant fluctuations on the surface, with things changing all the time. Most of the time, these surface-level experiences consume our attention without much awareness. We are driven unconsciously through thoughts and experiences, barely even noticing them. It takes some time and work to move down into the depths of the ocean— the underlying wholeness of who we are, our true identity in God.

When we practice mindfulness meditation, we tap into this deep ocean. As Christian mindfulness practitioners, we know this depth is God. Beneath the constant changes of life, we are learning to practice acceptance and to rest in something constant and solid and true. In connecting with God in the depths, we nurture a vibrant relationship with God.

Out of Control

Perhaps change is so hard for us because it reminds us how little control we have—and it's hard to let go of illusions of control. We want to believe that more things in life are sure than death and taxes. The truth is that there *is* something surer than death and taxes, and that is our utter dependence on God. We do not have true control over our destinies, and we do not have the power to make all of our dreams come true. When we make statements like "It's in God's hands now," we betray our belief that it was ever in our hands to begin with.

It's not that we have no control, but realistically our control is significantly constrained by factors such as individual brain capacity, the imprint of life experiences, and environmental factors. Any control that we do have is only in the present moment, in our choice of response to this present moment. We cannot change the past or the future, only the now. This is the messy reality of life.

Jesus knows about the messiness of this human journey, using the metaphor of being "born again" to describe spiritual growth (John 3:5–8). Birth is super messy and sometimes painful.

Babies are highly dependent on others during their birth; their participation in the process is only one component of a rather complicated event. Then, once they are born, they remain highly dependent for quite some time. Babies cannot feed themselves, control their bodily functions, change locations, or engineer the meeting of their emotional needs. They cannot understand where they are or what is happening to them, and they have no understandable framework for their experience.

Jesus's choice of a birth metaphor is notable. He does not describe our entrance into faith as a gateway of enlightenment or the result of well-developed wisdom cultivated over a lifetime of growth and practice. He compares it to being born. Evidently, we can expect this business of the Christian life to be one of messiness, pain, dependence, and uncertainty.

The practice of mindfulness is a tool for being present to this messy experience of rebirth as we lay aside our own fruitless striving and put ourselves in the competent hands of God, the master midwife. When we open ourselves up in this way to God's kingdom work through mindfulness practice, it is not because it always makes us feel great and competent. It is because birth is an incredible, beautiful, wild thing, and we are safe in God's hands.

As mindful Christians, we know God holds each moment. God provides what we need, as a parent provides for a newborn child—not always in the way or the time that we would like, but with care and skill. We are the created and the cared for in this equation; God is the creator and the sustainer. It is okay to acknowledge the limits of our control. Mindfulness practice helps us do this.

It is a radical act of faith to believe that if we turn toward our moment-to-moment experience with acceptance, Jesus is present with something to offer in the now. The silence of mindfulness meditation is often uncomfortable and difficult, with increased exposure to the stream of thoughts and feelings circling around the mind. And life itself is often uncomfortable and difficult. But Jesus is present, ready to heal whatever we are willing to bring to the light. We need not fear our thoughts and feelings; they are not in our control, but they are safe in the hands of the master.

Living the Practice: Welcoming Feelings

In this mindfulness practice, the goal is to practice awareness of emotions in the moment while holding a curious and welcoming attitude. We practice showing up for the present moment, regardless of which emotions are passing through.

Find a position that is both comfortable and alert. Close your eyelids either halfway or all the way, and take a couple of deep breaths. Then allow your breathing to return to its normal rhythm, and focus your attention on the body breathing itself. Get in touch with the sensations in your body—points of contact, areas of tightness or relaxation, sensations of blood flow or temperature. Give yourself some time here to settle into the feeling of your body.

Now allow your awareness to settle on your emotions. Notice your feelings and the quality of these feelings in your breath and body. See if it's possible to turn toward your emotions with an attitude of kindness. Notice that the feelings are present in the moment and also that they are passing phenomena—part of your experience that comes and goes, just like changing weather patterns. Practice accepting your feelings just as they are, noticing any resistant thoughts or urges that may arise toward the feelings and bringing your attention back to the emotions themselves.

If you choose, shift your body position into one that reflects your emotion in the moment. Is there a particular posture that expresses what you are feeling? Perhaps curled up into a ball or standing with arms raised high? Crying or smiling? Whatever it is, allow your body to enter into that posture as a full acceptance and expression of that emotion. Practice releasing any shame you might have about the feeling, and accept that where you are is where you are, noticing that the compassionate God is also with you in that emotion.

Once you have spent some time nurturing this accepting attitude toward your emotion, bring your practice to a close. Thank yourself for taking time to be authentic. Thank God for holding you in this moment of emotion, as God does in every other. ■

Sooner or later, we all discover that kindness
is the only strength there is.

—*Fr. Greg Boyle*[1]

CHAPTER 8

CLOTHED WITH COMPASSION

As a father has compassion for his children,
so the Lord has compassion for those who fear him.
Psalm 103:13

Common Humanity and Self-Compassion

Mindfulness brings us back to the basic human truth that we are all equal in the sight of God, who keeps no ranking system. When we practice nonjudgmental awareness of the present moment, we come back to the shared elements of being human: what we feel on our skin, what we hear in our ears, what we see with our eyes, what we taste in our mouths, what we smell through our noses. We also come back to the negative and fearful thinking patterns that plague the human brain. There is wide room in this awareness to learn the path of love as taught by Jesus.

These shared human experiences and connections are known in mindfulness language as "common humanity"—recognition that we are all on this human journey together. The gospel emphasizes this same theme, using language such as humility, justice, and grace to highlight our equal humanity. A related term common to the language of both mindfulness and Christian faith is compassion. Compassion allows us to treat one another with the kindness and respect with which we would all like to be treated, to pull together and experience common humanity along life's path.

While the theme of compassion has emerged repeatedly throughout this book, I'd like to drill down here into *self-compassion*,[2] which allows us to be participants in common humanity, treating ourselves with the kindness we would offer others on life's journey. Self-compassion is a core attitude throughout all formal and informal mindfulness practice, with particular emphasis in lovingkindness meditation (see chapter 4). Cultivating a sustained compassion for others requires creating a circle of compassion that includes ourselves. Without self-compassion, burnout becomes a significant risk for anyone in a helping role.

A compassionate response is quite typical when encountering the suffering of others, but for many, self-compassion can be the most challenging component of mindfulness. Can you remember the feeling in your heart when you last saw an injured child or a vulnerable kitten or a weeping friend? Chances are, there was some type of emotional, mental, and physical impulse to provide comfort. In contrast, kindness toward the self does not always come easily. When we are the ones hurting, our internal dialogue can sound more like "Get a grip! You're a mess." Most of us would rarely, if ever, talk that way to another human being.

Mindful self-compassion responds to our own suffering with internal dialogue that sounds more like "Ouch, I'm hurting." Self-compassion creates healthy habits of taking care of ourselves when we are in pain, turning toward our suffering with kindness, as we would toward a friend. It grounds us in the reality of common humanity, with a recognition that our suffering is a condition we share as human beings, rather than something that separates us.

The biblical book of Colossians provides a beautiful metaphor for the practice of compassion that covers both ourselves and others: "As God's chosen ones, holy and beloved, *clothe yourselves with compassion*, kindness, humility, meekness, and patience" (Col 3:12; emphasis added). Wearing compassion in this way—putting it on like clothing—implies that it is not only an outwardly expressed sentiment. It is also something meant for us, for the wearer of the garment. It surrounds us and protects us; it dresses us up and keeps us warm. Compassion is for others, and it is for the self, too. It is something for us to wear as God's chosen ones, holy and beloved.

Self-compassion mirrors the Christian concept of grace, an acknowledgment that there is nothing we can do to make God love us any more or any less.[3] Centuries of legalism within the Christian church have demonstrated how difficult it is for us to accept the gospel's emphasis on salvation by grace. We remain intent on proving our worth by doing enough good things and avoiding enough bad things. We really want to earn our salvation. Instead, God offers us grace—the assurance that we are completely loved exactly as we are.

We may feel squeamish about this, fearful that we're taking an easy way out. But the fact that so few of us really live in confidence of being loved shows that there is nothing easy about accepting grace. We would rather be in control of our worthiness. Scripture's encouragement that "there is no condemnation for those who are in Christ Jesus" (Rom 8:1–3) does not always sit well with us. Receiving grace through self-compassion is hard.

Practicing grace-filled self-compassion has several practical benefits. Self-compassion reduces fear of failure, knowing that kindness to self is an option when mistakes are made. This helps us take more risks and pursue life more wholeheartedly. Self-compassion provides freedom to apologize to others (and receive others' apologies) with an identity rooted in grace and not judgment. This injects our relationships with healthy humility, authenticity, and forgiveness. And self-compassion increases tolerance for painful emotion, as difficulties are wrapped in gentle care. This facilitates emotional healing and strengthens our resilience.

Another important benefit of self-compassion is that it creates the necessary foundation for mindful awareness. Without self-compassion, moment-to-moment awareness can be excruciating, filled with self-critical thoughts that trigger emotional pain. A self-compassionate attitude counters the lurking belief that life is hard because we are doing something wrong, that it is our fault we are struggling. It reminds us that we're having a hard time because life is hard, and it's okay to have a hard time doing something hard. This recognition that life is hard allows us to bring self-compassion into the reality of common humanity—the fact that no one gets through unscathed by suffering. And as Christians, we can be honest about our screwups and receive grace, knowing that God accepts us exactly as we are. When we make mistakes, we know we can clothe ourselves with God's compassion and live into the freedom of grace so clearly outlined in Scripture.

Beginning Again

The attitude of self-compassion lays a foundation for "beginner's mind." Beginner's mind is the freedom to begin again, over and over, whenever needed. It is an invitation to lay down baggage from the past—distant or immediate—that tries attaching itself to our identity. Employing beginner's mind, we can choose to see the present moment with fresh eyes, as if we had never seen it before, because as beginners, we haven't.

Saint Benedict is known for his saying, "Always we begin again." There is no better quote for the beginner's mind approach of mindfulness. Benedict knew that his long, detailed, legalistic, somewhat harsh set of requirements written for monks in the sixth century—the The Rule of Saint Benedict—could not be followed perfectly. Yet he also knew the freedom of receiving compassion and the fresh start inherent in each new moment: "Always we begin again."[4]

In mindfulness practice, beginner's mind supports the practitioner in stepping out of expert stance, which is a posture of all-knowing. In expert stance, we feel pressure to be right, smart, and respected; we are isolated from others because of our need for superiority. Expert stance keeps us thinking we have it all figured out. It closes us down to learning new things, blocking us from the experience of mystery.

Expert stance looks kind of like Job and his friends in the Old Testament. When Job is plunged into deep loss, his friends take thirty-three chapters of Scripture to think about, interpret, and analyze the situation. An expert stance like this is especially tempting during times of suffering. The more we hurt, the more we want to be in God's shoes—all-powerful and all-knowing—so we can figure out how to stop the hurt.

But beginner's mind looks different: it is the learner stance. When we are beginners, we bring our knowledge and skill while being open to growth in each moment. We recognize that each moment is brand-new to us, that there is always something to learn, no matter how familiar something feels. No moment is ever repeated in exactly the same way. Beginner's mind is a way of living into the mystery of the moment and the mystery of God.

In the story of Job, God silences Job and his expert friends with a reminder to shift into the learner stance of beginner's mind. Then they can hear that it is God who created the foundations of the world, who brings the sun up in the morning and sends it down at night, and who controls the tides of the ocean and knows the number of our days. God is God, and we are not. By the end of the story, what restores Job is his return to the not-knowing posture of a beginner. The book of Job is a testament to the power of humility, silence, and observation in the midst of suffering—to the power of beginner's mind.

As it did for Job, beginner's mind puts me back in the place of being small, vulnerable, and open before God. It highlights that the best path, even in the midst of suffering (or maybe especially then), is attunement to the awesome mystery of God's creation. Restoration comes from the humble acknowledgment that I don't know much in relation to God and from getting quiet enough to pay attention to the wonders going on around me. This lets me be a student; I am here to learn, practice, and receive.

Beginner's mind from a Christian perspective is not only an acknowledgment that God has done awesome things in the past, but also mindfully seeing what God is doing new in every single moment of our lives. "I am about to do a new thing," says God through the prophet Isaiah. "Now it springs forth, do you not perceive it?" (Isa 43:18–19). And again in Revelation, God says, "Behold, I am making all things new." (Rev 21:5). Are we here, right now, paying attention to the new? Or are we lost in perseverative thought and overanalysis? Are we ready to be silenced by our creator God? Are we humble enough to take a beginner's stance and to listen?

In any long-term relationship that matters to us—whether with God, family, friends, or significant others—we must cultivate this ability to start over. Beginner's mind enriches our relationships. The majority of our distress in relational conflict has to do with past and future thinking. In my own life, it does not take long in a marital dispute to resort to "You always do this" and "This will always be awful." This past and future thinking positions me in the "expert stance"; it puts me in a place of overthinking and attempting to be all-knowing. This is unhelpful to a conversation, unfair to my spouse, and painful for me. Beginner's mind brings me back to the present moment, starting over, noticing what is here, and allowing space for forgiveness. It is an attitude that asks with humility, "Can we start over?" It is choosing to be right here, right now, entering always into fresh beginnings.

Not every relationship should invite a continual starting over. In abusive situations, it is beneficial to observe toxic cycles and free ourselves from relationships that are causing harm. But in relationships where the basic blueprint is healthy, beginner's mind is just the tool we need to coexist in harmony. It allows us to self-soothe during times of relational stress and to give others the grace they need. It is the practice of forgiving "seventy times seven" that Jesus exhorts us to adopt (Matt 18:22). Beginner's mind helps us release our emotional grip on the past or fear of the future and to come into the present with people we care about.

Practically speaking, beginner's mind is implementing present-moment awareness in all the ways we have already explored in this book: paying attention to our physical sensations, thoughts, feelings, and other experiences in the present moment with open curiosity. By orienting our attention to these elements of the *now* through formal and informal mindfulness practices, we are allowing ourselves to begin again. It also can be helpful to add specific beginner's thoughts—for example, "I am beginning again. I am starting over. It is okay to let go of these thoughts about the past and come fresh to this moment. I am not defined by the past, and I do not need to understand everything. I am a beginner."

Jesus asked us to "receive the kingdom of God as a little child" (Mark 10:15), and surely this invitation to be a beginner is part of what he means. We have already explored the curiosity and surprise that are inherent in young children. Beginner's mind provides us with the opportunity to approach life with this childlike surprise, to watch in wonder and amazement as the world is rolled out before us, moment to moment. It lets us walk the journey of life in the same way that a two-year-old walks down a sidewalk, stopping to notice and examine and experience each thing with surprise: a stick! a leaf! a stone! a flag! It allows us to recognize that in each moment, we are experiencing something new that we have never before experienced. Embracing life as a beginner allows us to receive the new things that God is continually doing.

Living the Practice: Soaking in Grace

Self-compassion is a foundational attitude of both mindfulness practice and Christian theology, and it gives us permission to begin again, as often as needed. Adapted from a letter-writing exercise created by Dr. Kristin Neff,[5] the following practice places self-compassion within a framework of listening prayer. Here are some recommended steps:

1. Bring to mind a quality of yourself that you do not like, and take some time to write about it. Be honest about your thoughts and feelings, noticing any pain that might be present and allowing it to just be there, as much as you are able in the moment. When you are finished, set down your writing.

2. Close your eyes and take a deep breath. Notice that God is present as an all-loving, fully compassionate, unconditionally accepting being. Offer all you have written to God; there is no need to add more words or explanations. The goal is to simply sit in God's presence and listen to what God has to say from a place of divine compassion and grace.

3. When you are ready, write a letter to yourself from the perspective of God. God knows all that is on your heart and loves you in all of your human imperfections. God knows what you have been through, the history behind your struggle, and each of your strengths and weaknesses. God treasures you and loves you as a prized creation. God longs for your health and happiness. When God encourages you to change and grow, God is able and

willing to provide for your needs along the way. Covered by God's grace, you are accepted exactly as you are. Do your best to infuse your letter with this kind, caring, compassionate perspective that God has for you.

4. Take time to sit in silence and absorb the words on your paper, allowing them to sink in as you experience self-compassion—the compassion of God welling up from within. Put the letter down, but come back to it over time as a way to absorb the truth of God's unconditional love, acceptance, and grace.

5. Notice whether you need to slow the pace of this self-compassion practice. One of the challenges of the practice is that it begins with getting in touch with suffering, and this can sometimes lead to emotional flooding as we encounter repressed emotions. If that is the case for you, give yourself permission to engage with your letter-writing exercise in small doses that you return to as you are able. Slowing down self-compassion can itself be an act of self-compassion.

Sometimes we have complicated feelings about God, particularly as related to our pain. If linking to God through this practice feels like a barrier for you, consider writing your letter from the perspective of an imaginary unconditionally loving friend instead. God will be present and available anyway. ■

Listen to your life. See it for the fathomless mystery that it is. In the boredom and the pain of it no less than the excitement and gladness: touch, taste, smell your way to the holy and hidden heart of it because in the last analysis all moments are key moments, and life itself is grace.

—*Frederick Buechner*[1]

CHAPTER 9

THE TINY-YET-ENORMOUS KINGDOM

The kingdom of heaven is like a mustard seed that someone took and sowed in his field; it is the smallest of all the seeds, but when it has grown it is the greatest of shrubs and becomes a tree, so that the birds of the air come and make nests in its branches.

Matthew 13:31–32

Happiness

With all of the references to happiness in this book, it's time to make a deeper exploration of the topic to avoid some common misperceptions and pitfalls. The modern world has become chock-full of tips about how to be happy and live the good life. We strive to implement this trove of tips gleaned from the internet, self-help books, and a variety of podcasts, which give the general impression that we should have this figured out by now. In a world where we have so much good advice, why are we not happier?

Part of the difficulty is that we have come to believe that through all of these self-improvement measures, we should have feelings of happiness all the time. Unpleasant emotions are considered problems to be fixed, abnormalities in the human experience to be resolved. Chronic comparisons in the world of social media highlight reels have exacerbated this belief, as so many people on our screens appear to be happy. These inaccurate expectations of happiness lead to an overthinking of normal emotional fluctuations and to a retriggering of unhappy feelings. When we obsessively analyze our unpleasant emotional experiences, trying to explain why we feel so unhappy, our negative thinking loops lock in unhappiness.

No one feels happy all the time. As long as you are alive, your emotions will come and go, fluctuate and morph and transform. Happiness comes and goes, along with sadness, anger, joy, stress, excitement, grief, fear, and compassion. This is okay; it is normal. It means you are a human being. It also means, as we looked at earlier, that you are made in the image of God, who is shown in Scripture to experience the same range of emotions.

Cultivating happiness is hard for many of us because it means dropping resistance to unhappiness. It means accepting unpleasant emotion, leaning in and opening up to it. It even means welcoming that unpleasant emotion exactly as it is.

Earlier, I mentioned that when I first started mindfulness training, I was drawn to the metaphor of hospice. Here I had spent my whole life working so hard at trying to stop being depressed, and suddenly I was just supposed to accept it? To say, "Yes, I'm depressed, and it's out of my control," to lay it all down and admit I couldn't change it? That was not appealing, and I had to do some real grieving as I let go of my resistance to depressed feelings.

Fortunately, I've lived long enough to know the power of hospice care—to observe how acceptance in the face of death can open us to all kinds of beautiful things. And this was the reality of mindfulness for me: acceptance in the face of deep despair opened me up to happiness. I couldn't start with an expectation of happiness. I had to start with an acceptance of my feelings just as they were, moment to moment.

I'm a lot happier than I used to be. Giving up the struggle against unhappiness has created new room in my soul for joy. I no longer respond to my unhappy feelings as problems to be fixed, relating to them instead as transient emotional events that will come and go. In the same way, I choose not to cling to happy feelings, viewing them instead as passing phenomena to savor as they pass through. This process of curious acceptance, of mindfulness, has led me to the first consistent feelings of happiness I have experienced in my life. Mindfulness meditation and mindful awareness get me out of my head and into the joy that God has woven into the very fabric of our universe.

Sometimes in the Christian world, there can be pressure (internally or externally) to feel more happy than we actually do. Common children's songs in the church setting can reflect this expectation of happiness, and these can be somewhat confusing, painful, or even angering for people who are experiencing emotional suffering. Perhaps you are familiar with the song "Down in My Heart," which begins, "I've got the joy, joy, joy, joy down in my heart"; it's one example of many songs that seem to expect a "happy feeling" for Christians.

These songs used to bother me, but mindfulness has led me to view them differently. Rather than hearing them as descriptors of how I am expected to feel emotionally, I now see them as signs reminding me of what God has planted deep within: seeds of joy and happiness. These seeds are tended by my creator God, who loves me, and I do not need to manufacture well-being in order for them to be present. There is always happiness there within me, whether or not I feel it. The challenge is to become more attentive so that I can clear the distractions and uncover the qualities that God is nurturing down in my core.

So if happiness lies at our core, how do we get down to those happy feelings? We can get there through mindfulness meditation, time spent walking down the path to this place of "home" that lies deep within the jungle of our thoughts, feelings, physical sensations, behaviors, and urges. It is through mindfulness meditation that I know about this happy, sweet, quiet, beautiful, refreshing spot inside of my heart. God put it there, and it is my job to practice walking the path, so I can return to it on a regular basis.

Now when I am having a hard day, flooded by insecurity or anger or stress, I can more easily connect with what the song calls "joy down in my heart." I may or may not feel happy in the process, but the quiet stillness of God's provision exists on a much deeper level than my feelings. Knowing that the path to God's joy is there, I practice following it through the jungle of present-moment experiences.

The Kingdom of God

Happiness is just one small piece of the goodness permeating the universe. God has filled the world with God's good kingdom in so many ways, but we often don't see it in the midst of our mental distraction. We live with a type of spiritual blindness that keeps us from seeing the things around us, right in front of us. Even when Jesus was on earth, many were unable to see who he was, leading him to exclaim things like "Do you have eyes, and fail to see?" (Mark 8:18) on a regular basis.

When we practice mindfulness meditation, we are practicing *seeing* by meditating on what is right in front of us. We are practicing life with eyes wide open, fully engaged and alert. This helps us, as Christian practitioners, to observe and experience God's kingdom in the world, in both our individual lives and our corporate, relational lives together.

Once the Pharisees asked Jesus when the kingdom of God was coming, and he answered, "The kingdom of God is not coming with things that can be observed; nor will they say 'Look, here it is!' or 'There it is!' For, in fact, the kingdom of God is among [or within] you" (Luke 17:20–21). Most of us—or myself, for sure— would like a kingdom that can be observed in a more obvious way, with no more cancer, tsunamis, stillbirth, sexual abuse, or mental illness. But Jesus says the kingdom of God may not be that obvious to the human eye. It is actually among you, within you, already here, present, right now. It's just not always easy to see. Jesus describes the kingdom using metaphors of things that are tiny yet enormous: a mustard seed (Mark 4:30–32), yeast (Matt 13:33), and buried treasure (Matt 13:44). Mindfulness helps us to notice the tiny kingdom, so we are ready for the enormous payoffs along the way: the large tree, the leavened bread, the valuable treasure. It helps us to slow down and open ourselves to the kingdom.

Allow me to share a story of my own difficulty in seeing God's kingdom. I lost my first son (with a possible twin) to miscarriage at fourteen weeks. Then I lost a child at eight weeks, and then another set of twins at twelve weeks, and then another child at ten weeks. And then I lost a daughter to stillbirth at thirty-seven weeks. Grief became a way of life for me, a finely honed craft that I practiced day in and day out, a new normal that allowed me to keep up with my responsibilities but miss my children, too. I grappled with bitterness and a deep sense of not belonging, of being treated unfairly. I didn't see God as very good.

One night soon after my first loss, I tired of tossing and turning in bed and decided to take a midnight walk. It was September, and the streets of our small town were quiet. The air was warm, there was a gentle breeze. And as I walked under a tree (I remember the exact spot), I experienced an acute awareness of Jesus, suddenly and unexpectedly. He was with me, right beside me, closer than my breath. I have never forgotten the awe of that experience, and it helped to carry me through the many unanticipated losses to follow. God— "Emmanuel"—was with me (Matt 1:23). I had encountered the kingdom.

Three years later and eight months after my final pregnancy loss (the stillbirth of my daughter Elsa), I was struggling to see anything good in the midst of my grief journey. My husband and I had moved to a new city, and we visited a church where the sermon was on the kingdom of God. The pastor encouraged us to recognize that God's kingdom is here in the present moment, that we are living in it now. I hated that sermon. I was livid, in fact. "Really?" I found myself asking sarcastically. "This is it? This is God's kingdom? Frankly, it really sucks."

I have a lot of empathy for myself as I look back on that moment of pain. Grief, like so much of life, is really, really heart-wrenching and hard. I still have plenty of moments where my instinctual response is "I can't do this; it's too much," moments when God's kingdom seems like a million miles away. And I know that I'm not alone in this. Things like waterfalls and blue skies and random acts of kindness can seem much easier to fit within a Christian worldview than things like stillbirth and war and infidelity. It is our natural response to life to pick and choose which parts we call good and which we don't. It's not easy seeing God's kingdom in the midst of suffering.

As the journey of grief has evolved for me, I have found mindfulness to be the tool that opens my eyes to God's good kingdom, even in the midst of painful emotions. That pastor was right; the good news of God's kingdom is right here in the present moment, all the time. But it took mindfulness training to slow me down, turn me toward the moment, connect me with my full experience, and tune my senses so I could see God's gifts. As in that midnight encounter with Jesus's presence after my first loss, the reality of God's kingdom is right here all the time, and mindful awareness helps me notice.

The focus here has been on seeing God's kingdom in individual moments of mindful awareness, but that does not mean this is a practice done only in isolation. Mindfulness practice can be a powerful source of connection with others, and even the individual practices of mindfulness help us to experience God's kingdom in its corporate manifestation as well. In fact, university students completing exit surveys after participating in my mindfulness training group almost always report increased feelings of connection with others. Mindfulness meditation helps them cultivate and value the community around them. This was true for me in my own healing journey after pregnancy loss, as God's kingdom showed up communally through the support of friends and family. Mindfulness practice allowed me to see and receive these gifts of the kingdom—the love, comfort, and simple presence that God provided through the people around me.

It's important to remember that noticing God's kingdom is different from thinking about it, describing it, or even expounding on it as I have done in this chapter. Cognitive frameworks such as what we are exploring in this book can be helpful in preparing for mindfulness practice, but mindful awareness is not an analytic cognitive practice. Rather, it is a practice of curious observation as we directly experience what is available in each moment, moving us off the speeding train of thoughts so we can dwell more directly with our experience. And we Christians know each present-moment experience to exist within the borders of God's good, tiny-yet-enormous kingdom.

Living the Practice: Visiting from Mars

One practical way of increasing present-moment awareness is to activate surprise, implementing the beginner's mind discussed in chapter 8 as a method of engaging with the tiny-yet-enormous kingdom discussed in this chapter. Let's try it out.

Pretend that you are a Martian who has just landed. You have never been in this place before, or anything like it. You are curious about what you see; this is all brand-new, and you're not sure what to make of it all. You might ask yourself questions such as these:

- What shapes and colors do I notice?

- What sounds do I hear?

- Am I experiencing any smells or tastes?

- What is coming in through my sense of touch?

None of this has "meaning" yet, because it is so brand-new. You are simply observing with curiosity, taking it in as if for the very first time. If it feels like too much to take in all at once, narrow your observation down to one specific object in your environment—maybe a chair or book or food item.

In this moment, you are not an expert on your environment. You are starting from scratch. You do not have a history to filter through or cloud your perception. You are ready to learn, beginning with simple observations of this novel world in which you have found yourself. What do you notice through the eyes of a beginner?

Practice sitting with this attitude of beginner's mind for several minutes, laying aside interpretations and expectations related to your environment in order to be present with your moment-to-moment experience in a more direct way. Treat this moment, smack-dab in the middle of God's kingdom, as if you have never experienced it before and have much to learn—because you haven't, and you do. ∎

Do not be in a hurry. Know that no matter
how hard you push, you cannot push
yourself beyond where you are,
just as you are, in the present moment.
Nor do you need to.

—James Finley[1]

CHAPTER 10

BEING CHRISTIAN, MINDFULLY

In returning and rest you shall be saved;

in quietness and trust shall be your strength.

Isaiah 30:15

Reading about mindfulness meditation will not teach you to meditate; only meditating teaches that. The doorway into the gifts of mindfulness will be consistent engagement with the practice, beginning with the practices of formal mindfulness meditation.

The good news is that you don't need to be a meditation guru to reap the benefits of mindfulness. I know people who meditate every day and live with an enviable serenity and centeredness. Others reach for formal mindfulness practices occasionally during times of stress to find equilibrium and restoration as needed. My practice is much more of the latter.

In my case, I struggle to maintain self-care routines. Exercising regularly, eating my vegetables, and maintaining prayer routines do not come easily for me. I've been known to numb out on social media during times of stress instead of reaching out for support, and my journal of late is looking pretty blank. This lack of routine defines my meditation practice as well.

Yet the powerful simplicity of mindfulness has been life-changing for me. It turns out that God can use mindfulness within a variety of application styles to transform us and open us up into people who experience joy. While wholehearted and consistent engagement with formal mindfulness meditation was crucial for me at the beginning of my mindfulness journey, my practice now is sustained on a more ongoing basis by the frequent application of informal mindful awareness each day. This is only my unique mindfulness story; your story will be uniquely yours.

Knowing how much mindfulness to practice is much like learning how much food to eat or how much water to drink. There are many guidelines for such practices, such as counting calories and setting goals for water intake each day, but any sound nutritionist will tell you that the true goal is to listen to the body's signals of hunger and thirst each day. Paying attention to our natural, God-given indicators leads to effective regulation of food and water. Am I hungry? Am I thirsty? Can I feel that this food is providing me with needed energy and nutrients, or is there something different that my body needs in this moment?

So it is with mindfulness. Guidelines and goals for formal meditation are helpful, and a daily practice of mindfulness meditation is a powerful tool for wellness. But for those who struggle to maintain that type of daily routine, be encouraged that the most important goal is to listen to your needs—to become aware of when your mind, body, and soul are thirsty for silence.

Not sure yet what it feels like to self-regulate your mindfulness practice or to thirst for silence? No worries! This is learned incrementally. At the beginning, establishing some type of mindfulness routine can be helpful. Perhaps you could schedule one guided mindfulness meditation per day or attend a mindfulness meditation class that meets regularly for structure, accountability, and support. Over time, your God-given systems of self-regulation will be strengthened as you practice paying attention, and knowing how and when to implement mindfulness will become easier. Along the way, you are invited to be patient with yourself, practicing self-compassion in the process of figuring out your own mindful rhythm over time.

Mindfulness is a beautiful practice for anyone seeking to go deeper in life, to cultivate joy, to navigate pain, and to connect with God's presence. It is a receiving practice of intentional awareness in the present moment, placing us in the pathway to notice God's good kingdom gifts. It is an opening practice of listening, creating the conditions to hear God's voice. It is a nonresistant practice of acceptance, helping us release our tight grip in acknowledgment that only God is sovereign. It is a seeing practice, clearing our vision so that we can live life fully in tune with God's glorious creation.

Mindfulness moves us out of worry and distraction, wakes us up to resurrection life, and connects us with God's presence at the joyful core of who we are. It quiets the din of self-absorbed thoughts, turning our attention toward self and others with kind compassion. It helps us extend forgiveness, receive grace, and feel better.

Mindfulness is, ultimately, a God-given gift.

May mindfulness inspire you to walk to the entrance of the cave and attend to the silence, as Elijah did in the wilderness. May it allow you to sit at Jesus's feet without distraction, as Mary did in the midst of Martha's worried bustle. May it become an occasion for you to bring all that is available to Jesus, as Andrew did in the hungry crowd. May mindfulness foster curiosity about how God is providing for you in each moment, make visible the goodness of God's creation within yourself and all around you, and engender life-giving humility before your maker. May mindfulness be a practice for cultivating intentionality, openness, and faith as you walk the path of Jesus with trust and confidence in his provision.

God is right here, right now, in the present moment. Let's practice being here, too.

Living the Practice: Looking Ahead

You've made it this far. You've read the book, thought about the integration of mindfulness and Christian faith, and maybe even done some of the practices along the way. What's next?

Set aside some time in God's presence for intentional planning of your own mindful Christian walk.

- Consider your mindfulness practice so far, identifying what would support you in taking the next step. Perhaps you would like to schedule an intentional practice time each day, take a mindfulness class, or join with others who are already engaging in the practice.

- Consider whether professional support, such as a therapist or support group, would also be helpful for you as you learn to navigate challenging patterns of thought, feeling, and/ or behavior in your life through mindfulness practice.

- Through the process, listen for God's guiding voice.

If you have remaining questions about the integration of mindfulness and Christian faith, you might use a journal to record your thoughts about these. Consider seeking out wise counsel from people in your life who pursue contemplation as a spiritual discipline.

Then set out on the next leg of your mindfulness journey, knowing that God goes with you every step of the way.

God beneath you,

God in front of you,

God behind you,

God above you,

God within you.

WITH GRATITUDE

So many people and places have helped to make this book happen!

Thanks to Ken for bringing me wildflowers and edible treats while I wrote and for encouraging me every step along the way, and thanks to Milo for leaving me sweet notes that said, "You can do it" exactly when I needed them. I love you both. Your kindness, wisdom, and humor warm my heart every day.

Thanks to my editors—to Silas Morgan for asking me to write the book and to Lil Copan for helping to shape my runaway words into something worth reading. I couldn't have done this without you.

Thanks to April Kaiserlian of the Grand Rapids Center for Mindfulness for teaching me mindfulness and for creating calm, healing spaces. Your authenticity and presence have been a gift.

Thanks to the students of Calvin University for sitting with me in mindful silence over the past six years and to the members of Grace Church who have engaged wholeheartedly with this practice. You've given me the inspiration, challenge, and focus I needed to formulate my ideas around mindful Christianity.

Thanks to readers of The Mindful Christian website, who let me know that this book was relevant and needed. Please keep sending me notes.

Thanks to the beautiful people of Stovetop Roasters for keeping me caffeinated and entertained through the many seasons of writing. You make really good vanilla lattes.

Thanks to God for filling all the moments of life with goodness and then teaching me to pay attention. I'm all yours!

ENDNOTES

1   F. R. Shapiro, "Who Wrote the Serenity Prayer?," *Chronicle Review*, April 28, 2014, https://tinyurl.com/y28c2ssl.

CHAPTER 1

1   Mother Teresa, *No Greater Love* (Novato, CA: New World Library, 1997), 10.

CHAPTER 2

1   Desmond Tutu, quoted by Richard Rohr as a personal communication in "The Will of God," *Daily Meditations* (blog, Center for Action and Contemplation), June 20, 2016, https://tinyurl.com/y2kz5ldm. Falling Upward: A Spirituality for the Two Halves of Life by Richard Rohr, 2011, Jossey-Bass, San Francisco, page ix.

2   James Baraz, personal communication, August 26, 2015.

3   Siri Chandler, "How to Explain Mindfulness to Young Children," Mindfulness for Children, April 24, 2012, https://tinyurl.com/yxvlfztj

4   Tom Ireland, "What Does Mindfulness Meditation Do to Your Brain?," *Scientific American* (guest blog), June 12, 2014, https://tinyurl.com/y66ffqxy.

5   W. Kuyken, F. C. Warren, R. S. Taylor, et al., "Efficacy of Mindfulness-Based Cognitive Therapy in Prevention of Depressive Relapse: An Individual Patient Data Meta-analysis from Randomized Trials," *JAMA Psychiatry* 73, no. 6 (2016): 565–74, doi:10.1001/jamapsychiatry.2016.0076.

6   Jennifer Wolkin, "How the Brain Can Change Your Experience of Pain," *Mindful*, April 28, 2016, https://tinyurl.com/y29q5k7x.

7   Greg Boyle, "The Calling of Delight: Gangs, Service, and Kinship," interview by Krista Tippett, *On Being*, February 26, 2013, updated November 22, 2017, https://tinyurl.com/y2puesq8.

8   The first part of the quote comes from Annie Dillard, *Pilgrim at Tinker Creek* (New York: Harper & Row, 1985), 10. The second part comes from Annie Dillard, The Meaning of Life: Reflections in *Words and Pictures on Why We Are Here*, ed. David Friend (Boston: Little, Brown, 1991), 11.

CHAPTER 3

1 Rebecca Harding Davis, "Thanksgiving," *Independent* 57, no. 2 (November 24, 1904): 1196.

2 Matthew Fox, trans. and commentator, *Breakthrough: Meister Eckhart's Creation Spirituality in New Translation* (Garden City, NY: Doubleday, 1980).

3 Jean-Pierre de Caussade, *The Sacrament of the Present Moment* (San Francisco: Harper & Row, 1982).

4 James Martin, *A Jesuit Guide to (Almost) Everything: A Spirituality for Real Life* (New York: HarperOne, 2010).

5 Thomas Keating, *Open Mind, Open Heart: The Contemplative Dimension of the Gospel* (New York: Amity House, 1986).

6 Thomas Keating, *The Method of Centering Prayer: The Prayer of Consent* (Butler, NJ: Contemplative Outreach, 2016), retrieved from Contemplative Outreach at https://tinyurl.com/y27v5agu.

7 Dallas Willard, *Hearing God: Developing a Conversational Relationship with God* (Downers Grove, IL: InterVarsity, 2012).

8 Brother Lawrence, *The Practice of the Presence of God the Best Rule of a Holy Life* (New York: Fleming H. Revell, 1895).

9 James D. Bratt, ed., *Abraham Kuyper: A Centennial Reader* (Grand Rapids: Eerdmans, 1998), 488.

10 Barbara Brown Taylor, *Learning to Walk in the Dark* (New York: HarperOne, 2014).

CHAPTER 4

1 Thomas Merton, *Thoughts in Solitude* (New York: The Noonday Press, 1956), 93.

2 Jon Kabat-Zinn, "Mindfulness-Based Interventions in Context: Past, Present, and Future," *Clinical Psychology: Science and Practice* 10, no. 2 (2003): 144–56.

3 *Encyclopedia Britannica*, s.v. 'Information Theory,' by George Markowsky, June 16, 2017, https://tinyurl.com/y6t8l904.

4 A. Mehrabian, *Silent Messages* (Oxford: Wadsworth, 1971).

5   Timothy Keller, *The Prodigal God: Recovering the Heart of the Christian Faith*
    (New York: Riverhead, 2008).

6   Y. Sheu, L. H. Chen, and H. Hedegaard, *Sports- and Recreation-Related Injury
    Episodes in the United States, 2011–2014*, National Health Statistics Reports,
    no. 99 (Hyattsville, MD: National Center for Health Statistics, 2016).

7   L. Xiaochen, X. Zhang, J. Guo, et al., "Effects of Exercise Training on
    Cardiorespiratory Fitness and Biomarkers of Cardiometabolic Health: A
    Systematic Review and Meta-analysis of Randomized Controlled Trials,"
    Journal of the American Heart Association 4, no. 7 (July 17, 2015), retrieved
    from https://tinyurl.com/yyvqry2d.

8   M. Farias and C. Wikholm, "Has the Science of Mindfulness Lost
    Its Mind?," *BJPsych Bulletin* 40, no. 6 (2016): 329–32, doi:10.1192/
    pb.bp.116.053686.

CHAPTER 5

1   Elizabeth Barrett Browning, Aurora Leigh, 1857, in D. H. S. Nicholson
    and A. H. E. Lee, eds., *The Oxford Book of English Mystical Verse* (Oxford:
    Clarendon, 1917).

2   S. Marek and N. Dosenbach, "The Frontoparietal Network: Function,
    Electrophysiology, and Importance of Individual Precision Mapping,"
    Dialogues in Clinical Neuroscience 20, no. 2 (2018): 133–40.

3   A. Manoliu, C. Meng, F. Brandl, A. Doll, M. Tahmasian, et al., "Insular
    Dysfunction within the Salience Network Is Associated with Severity of
    Symptoms and Aberrant Inter-network Connectivity in Major Depressive
    Disorder," *Frontiers in Human Neuroscience* 7, no. 930 (2014), doi:10.3389/
    fnhum.2013.00930.

4   J. F. Coutinho, S. V. Fernandesl, J. M. Soares, et al., "Default Mode Network
    Dissociation in Depressive and Anxiety States," *Brain Imaging and Behavior*
    10, no. 147 (2016), https://doi.org/10.1007/s11682-015-9375-7.

5   A. M. Mowinckel, D. Alnæs, M. L. Pedersen, S. Ziegler, M. Fredriksen,
    et al., "Increased Default-Mode Variability Is Related to Reduced Task-
    Performance and Is Evident in Adults with ADHD," *NeuroImage: Clinical* 16
    (2017): 369–82, doi:10.1016/j.nicl.2017.03.008.

6   John M. Gottman and Nan Silver, *The Seven Principles for Making Marriage
    Work* (New York: Crown, 1999).

7   Mark Williams and Danny Penman, *Mindfulness: An Eight-Week Plan for Finding Peace in a Frantic World* (Emmaus, PA: Rodale, 2011).

8   Melinda B. Clark-Gambelunghe and David A. Clark, "Sensory Development," *Pediatric Clinics* 62, no. 2 (April 2015): 367–84.

CHAPTER 6

1   Ann Voskamp, *One Thousand Gifts: Dare to Live Fully Right Where You Are* (HarperCollins Publishing, 2011), 57.

2   Vocabulary.com Dictionary, s.v. "curiosity," accessed July 15, 2019, https://tinyurl.com/y4k3v3jl.

CHAPTER 7

1   Barbara Brown Taylor, *An Altar in the World: A Geography of Faith* (New York: HarperOne, 2009).

2   Sonja Lyobomirsky, *The How of Happiness: A New Approach to Getting the Life You Want* (New York: Penguin, 2007).

3   Brené Brown, *Daring Greatly: How the Courage to Be Vulnerable Transforms the Way We Live, Love, Parent, and Lead* (New York: Gotham, 2012).

4   Frederich Buechner, *The Final Beast* (New York: HarperCollins, 1965).

5   Wendell Berry, "Manifesto: The Mad Farmer Liberation Front," in *The Country of Marriage* (San Diego: Harcourt Brace Jovanovich, 1973).

6   Lyobomirsky, *The How of Happiness*.

CHAPTER 8

1   Greg Boyle, *Tattoos on the Heart: The Power of Boundless Compassion* (New York: Free Press, 2010).

2   Kristin Neff, *Self-Compassion: The Proven Power of Being Kind to Yourself* (New York: William Morrow, 2011).

3   Philip Yancey, *What's So Amazing about Grace?* (New York: HarperCollins, 1997).

4   Benedict of Nursia, *The Rule of St. Benedict*, trans. Anthony C. Meisel and M. L. del Mastro (Garden City, NY: Image, 1975).

5   Neff, *Self-Compassion*.

CHAPTER 9

1   Frederick Buechner, *Now and Then: A Memoir of Vocation* (New York: HarperCollins, 1991).

CHAPTER 10

1   James Finley, *Christian Meditation: Experiencing the Presence of God* (San Francisco: HarperSanFrancisco, 2004).